The Rainmaking Mindset

For Attorneys

Attracting Clients, Winning Business, and Increasing Profits

by Liz Wendling

Women & Co Press
Littleton, CO

The Rainmaking Mindset

For Attorneys

ISBN: 978-0-9846766-9-9

Website: www. therainmakingmindset.com
E-mail: liz@lizwendling.com

Printed in U.S.A.
Published by Women & Co Press
4385 South Balsam Street
Suite 11-201
Littleton, CO 80123

First Edition

Edited by Paulette K. Kinnes
Cover and interior design by Maryann Brown

Dedicated to my loving family, the most important people in my life. Your special love and humor feeds my soul.

Table Of Contents

Foreword

What you have in your hands is a masterpiece of essential information for you, the lawyer who currently uses the hope method of generating business. **Hope is not the strategy of choice for most lawyers that I know**. The phone does not ring by magic. Getting out there and doing something makes the phone ring.

As a lawyer who has practiced for decades, I would tell you that there is not a day that goes by that I do not sell my services and myself to prospective clients.

I think that the secret, however, is not to think of it as selling. I do not like to sell. Selling feels pushy and phony to me. I can recognize someone who is not sincere from a mile away.

But I love what I do, and knowing how I have been able to help my clients, I view the selling part of my business as critical to building strong foundations with new clients. I think that my sincerity comes through with each discussion that I have, and I feel great knowing that my clients are protected as they start and grow their ventures.

I generally don't view my business-development activities as selling at all. I simply share information that may be useful to entrepreneurs everywhere.

Get out of your own way! It's a new world in which we are practicing. There are many professionals in every field, and those who win the trust and the business of each client are those who love what they do and like who they do it for.

The journey that you are about to embark upon with Liz may result in a major shift in your life, not to mention your law practice. The principals that she suggests will be effective not only in your practice, they will help you genuinely connect with people. All she asks is that you do the work. So, hunker down and evaluate your attitude. Adjust that attitude if need be.

Remember that if you love what you do, you never work a day in your life. Likewise, you never sell anything, either. You are eager to share out of a sense of helpfulness to others.

But the key is that you must take action! You cannot sit back and hope for something to happen. The chapters in this book should be read, re-read, and then acted upon. There is never success without trying!

If we were all great at sales, no one would need a book such as this one. Since there are no classes in law school about how to sell your services, most graduates believe that after law school comes a job with a firm. Graduates believe that it is the job of that firm to bring in the work in some mystical manner and that they are there to do the work that is brought in by the business fairy.

Sales take training. Attitudes, beliefs, actions, and systems all point you toward success. What you think you can do is always correct. And what you think you can do is a matter of attitude.

Rainmaking is a skill set. And it's a skill set that is completely new for most attorneys. We need to be open to different ways of doing things.

In this book, Liz aims to help you break free of self-limiting beliefs and to stop seeing the world as half empty. Business today is about approaching people in the way that you would like to be approached. The information that Liz presents here will be easy to implement.

I'm thrilled that you are making the effort to learn new ways of making rain. If you follow the suggestions made by Liz in this magnificent book, your future will be bright. Make it a regular practice to review the principals in each chapter over and over again until they become second nature to you.

Best of luck to you.

Stephen Replin
www.ReplinLawGroup.com

Introduction

Successful rainmakers are made, not born. Rainmakers are a rare breed. Rainmaking is a learned skill, not an inherited trait. This is not a myth, it is the truth. Certain people seem to have an innate ability to connect and communicate with others in a warm, natural, and spontaneous way. While those gifts give them a strong advantage, they are not enough to transform someone into an accomplished rainmaker.

Rainmakers possess a skill and an ability that differentiates them from the pack and the competition. This skill is sales! Rainmakers are confident and comfortable with selling. They know that they have to sell and choose to get good at it. They understand how to strike client- and business-development gold. Making it rain is synonymous with selling, marketing, and networking activities.

Attorneys who know how to sell earn more money. They know how to make rain in any and all conditions.

Many people carry a ton of baggage related to the idea of sales and selling. Some people must resort to calling it something else in order to do it. They call it serving, sharing, educating, or helping. When they use those words, I say, *That IS selling. Selling is serving, sharing, educating, and helping*. Surprise! You are already doing what you have been fighting. Selling is not something that you do to someone. It is a collaborative process in which you help the client make a decision that will enable her to achieve her objective.

Others proclaim, *I'm not a natural-born salesperson. I don't like to sell. I didn't go into law to have to sell.*

Businesses fail constantly because people don't know how to sell or flat-out refuse to sell. Selling is often the last skill that people learn, instead of making it one of the first.

Selling is not about manipulating, convincing, or forcing someone to hire you. Selling is about understanding how prospects make their buying decisions and providing them with the information and guidance that they need to make an informed choice. I am here to help you make sure that that choice is to hire you.

It is time to drop the negative energy around the only thing that keeps your practice alive and thriving: sales.

Rainmaking is like sports. It is beneficial to have natural ability, but it is the combination of desire, effort, and dedication that makes a champion. You have the ability to sell inside you, and I am here to help you activate it.

Rainmaking allows you to be selective about those with whom you work. You choose to work with clients who are a perfect fit for you and/or your firm, as opposed to working with clients who turn out to be the wrong fit and a giant pain in the ass. We've all had a few of those. I hope that you have learned how to spot them early on. I know that I have.

Contrary to popular belief, there is no personality type or gender that makes a good rainmaker. There is also no single approach or method that makes rainmaking easier. However, there is a common thread that ties the rainmakers whom I know and have worked with together. They were bold and brave, driven and decisive, committed and consistent. They were ready to stop making excuses and start making rain.

These attorneys know that when they develop and strengthen their sales muscles, they will possess a valuable skill that so many other attorneys lack.

It won't be easy to make changes in your habits and routines. But if you want to be a rainmaker and win more business, you must step out of your comfort zone and do something different. Everyone has a next level of success, whether they are just starting out or are already eminently prosperous.

There is no shortage of books, programs, and systems available to you about how to build a lucrative practice, and there are countless ways to learn how to sell effectively and numerous ideas for forming a strong marketing message.

Each one has something that will help you learn and grow. But to fully understand and maximize the benefits from these endless choices, you first need to know the underlying principles and fundamentals of selling. And you need to know how to take what you learn and use it every day in your practice so that you may earn the rewards that you deserve.

You may be wondering what I could know about working with attorneys because I am not one. But I would tell you that I am also not a dentist, an accountant, a web designer, a chiropractor, a nutritionist, a financial planner, a plastic surgeon, an architect, or a real estate agent. However, I have worked with people in all of these professions. Every professional must actively market their services and sell themselves if they want to be profitable.

I excel in coaching and teaching all types of professionals, not just attorneys, because I understand people and human behavior. I know your clients and what they appreciate when meeting you. I know what turns them toward you and what turns them away from you. I know what they need when it comes to hiring you and understand why they don't. And finally, I know precisely what they look for when making a buying decision. That is why I wrote *The Rainmaking Mindset For Attorneys*.

I have chosen to focus part of my practice on coaching attorneys and designing programs just for them. I empower them to step up and be daring when marketing their services and selling themselves and to do it in a way that feels right and moves others to action.

I have designed programs that inspire attorneys to become more courageous and stronger in their practice and client-development process. I show them how to devise a robust system for forming, nurturing, and sustaining relationships with prospects, clients, and business partners. Once these skills are rock-solid and baked into their DNA, their income and profits skyrocket. They become rainmakers.

I encourage you to read this book in its entirety first. You may scan the book, skip over paragraphs, and speed-read through the chapters that you need the most, but that will be a waste of your time. You may even think, *Her ideas won't work in my practice. I tried that before and it failed. My practice is different.*

Decide right now that you are more interested in making rain than in making excuses. Make the choice that you are more devoted to your achievements than you are to those excuses (even really good ones). I am not asking you to try all of the suggestions at once. I encourage you to implement them at a pace that is realistic for you. Try one new idea. Get comfortable with it. Then try another, and another. And continue until your skills eventually evolve to a higher level of performance.

Chapter One
Business As Usual Is Over

Welcome to the new normal. As our world changes, the nature of business and relationships is changing too. Learning new ways of doing business will allow you to boost, refine, and scale your practice rapidly. Relying on relationship-building techniques developed five or ten years ago will only get you one thing: left behind.

Unfortunately, what worked reasonably well a decade ago is now miserably outdated and inadequate. Sticking with old-school techniques means leaving money on the table and making little rain. It also means that while you keep to the status quo, your competition is learning these new techniques.

When you choose to incorporate some of these fresh ideas into your sales and marketing efforts, you will be among the first to do so in your profession. And I can assure you that there are enormous competitive advantages in being first.

The marketplace is getting noisier and more crowded. There are many attorneys competing for the same clients and the same business. To rise above the noise and the competition, you must do something different, something that will make you stand out. That something different means that you need to be good at sales and marketing. It is no longer sufficient to simply be a smart attorney.

Learning how to market your services and sell yourself will increase the odds that you and/or your firm will win the business. You must be as comfortable marketing and selling as you are practicing law. Develop your practice by choice, not chance.

I tell all of my clients that it's important to know their product or service, but it's more important to know themselves and the value that they bring to the table.

The Internet and social media have completely, permanently, and radically changed the way that people connect, communicate, socialize, share, and conduct business. Everybody in every industry is now tapping into the mighty engine that is the Internet.

If you have not yet done this, you still have time. These days, not being on social media will send a loud and clear message to your prospective client that you have not evolved and that you have not gone with the flow of the ever-changing times.

For example, not being on and using LinkedIn is the equivalent of not being in the yellow pages two decades ago. People used to go to the yellow pages to find an attorney. Not anymore. Now they go to Google or another search engine. How will people find you if you are not actively putting yourself, your brand, and your practice out there for people to find, online and offline? Visibility generates credibility. Credibility increases profitability.

You may have read other books about sales and marketing. Many of those books talk about specific techniques and tricks that are centered around you and your agenda. They are filled with outdated scripts, clever questions, one-liners, and ways to close. They're full of superficial tips that feel forced, unnatural, and uncomfortable.

These tips and techniques no longer work on today's consumer. Why? Because they have been around for forty or fifty years, and everyone knows them. They worked then, they were perfect for that era, but not now. Selling and marketing have evolved. Now it is your turn.

Your job is to utilize the strategies and insights found in this book in your practice. Take what you read and put it into play, changing your mindset and behaviors in order to increase revenue.

If your goal is to be a rainmaker and grow a profitable business, it is time to develop your plan. You are in full control of what does and does not happen in your practice. Success is not promised to any of us, but it is available to all of us.

Many attorneys dodge the most important things that keep their practice in business. Below are the dirty half-dozen.

1. They don't know how to efficiently and effectively market their services and sell their expertise.
2. They would rather practice law than devote time and energy to business-development activities.
3. They are fearful and/or not willing to face the rejection that is inherent in business development.
4. They think that their reputation should speak for itself and that they should not have to go after the business.
5. They have a negative mindset about what sales and marketing are, so they sidestep them altogether.
6. They think that they have to turn into a stereotypical sales person, into someone that they're not to acquire a new client. They believe that they have to use pressure tactics to close the sale or fear that if they ask for the business, they will appear too pushy.

If your services are perceived as a commodity, it will be extremely difficult to get yourself in front of a steady stream of qualified potential clients who see you as different.

This book is the intersection of networking, marketing, and selling (business development) that enables you to broaden your practice in a way that feels good to you and your clients. My goal is not to turn you into a slick sales person or marketing guru. My goal is to provide you with the skills and the tools that you need to become highly effective at winning more business, painlessly and systematically.

I know that this is possible because the thousands of clients with whom I have worked have done it. They have paved the way for you. They were skeptical about trying a new approach but did it anyway and delivered results. They became rainmakers. If they can do it, so can you. Open your heart and mind to the possibilities.

As essential as the content in this book is, you still have some skills to learn and processes to establish. Roll up your sleeves, and let's make some rain together.

Chapter Two

Change Your Mindset, Change Your Results

If you can't make it rain, you can't grow your practice. Most attorneys are quite talented when it comes to practicing law, but unfortunately they don't know how to differentiate themselves and market and sell their services in a way that yields substantial results. There was no class in law school that taught them how to seamlessly integrate marketing and sales into their practice. Client and Business Development 101 did not exist.

Learning how to sell yourself first will not only change your income, it will change your practice and the way that your clients perceive you. Extraordinary benefits and increased income come from knowing how to sell effectively.

Selling is still a dirty word to many attorneys. With love I say, *get over it.* Everyone sells something, including you!

Attorneys at the top of their game recognize that to be good at client and business development, they need to make it a priority. They must work at it every day, treating selling activities with the same level of importance as their client work. Business development is a mindset as well as an activity.

Selling doesn't have to have a negative connotation. It is not about tricking, trapping, or pressuring people. Selling is a conversation, or a series of conversations, designed to help the client better understand the problem or issues that he is facing, and if you can help him, to inspire him to hire you by presenting your offering as irresistibly as possible.

Many attorneys lose opportunities strictly as a result of bucking the process and refusing to sell. They stand firm in their belief that they went to law school to practice law, not spend time selling their services. Resistance is what keeps them stuck and not maximizing their earning potential. This is precisely where changing your mindset will change your results.

Selling is getting harder every day. Competition is more intense than it used to be. There are more firms competing for the same business. You are meeting clients who have less time, less money, and shorter attention spans than ever before.

It's harder to get your foot in the door and even harder to make your message stick in your client's mind. You can't afford to NOT know how to sell. Get used to me beating that particular dead horse in the pages of this book.

Lean into the process of selling instead. Learn the formula for building a strong practice. And by the way, it is not a secret. There are no magic formulas to losing weight or saving money. It's pretty simple: eat less, move more; spend less, save more. Everyone knows the formula for both losing weight and saving money, but there are plenty of people who do neither. Remaining chubby and being broke is easier than doing the work that it takes to be healthy and manifest abundance.

Sell myself? Market my services? Not me! I have never had a single attorney yet tell me that they couldn't wait to hit the streets, pound the pavement, and sell and market their services. Not one. Clients are the lifeblood of an attorney's practice. Without clients, there is no practice...and no profits.

Can We Call It Something Else?

Recently I was hired to work with a team of divorce attorneys. During day one of training, the managing partner pulled me aside for a short meeting. He asked me to do something that I was not comfortable doing and frankly had never been asked to do before. He requested that I not use the words *sales, selling, or marketing* during the training, as he felt that the training would go much smoother if I refrained from using these loaded words.

I was told that all of the attorneys hated the entire notion of selling and marketing, and the managing partner preferred not to upset the apple cart. I was instructed to call it winning business, retaining clients, making rain, getting hired, and sealing the deal. Anything but what it really was, sales and business-development training. I was almost speechless.

I pushed back and asked him if the goal of the training was to inspire the attorneys to become rainmakers or to maintain the status quo? I stated that if I didn't get to the root of the problem, I was simply adding fuel to the fire of the revenue issue, or the non-revenue issue, as the case may be. I maintained that the sales problem would continue to grow out of control unless and until we called it what it was.

I needed the attorneys to own the fact that they must be comfortable in a selling role. I wanted them to change their mindset and adjust their thinking so that they could increase their profits. If they didn't buy the fact that they are selling themselves and their services, neither will their prospects.

I declared, "You hired me because your attorneys are struggling to win business. That is a sales issue! You hired me because the attorneys are uncomfortable selling themselves and not assertively asking for the business. That is a mindset issue!

"Your attorneys don't believe that they have to sell and have huge amounts of internal conflict around selling. Their resistance is causing resistance in the prospect, and that is why they are not closing sales. Uncomfortable people don't buy. Uncomfortable prospects won't hire your firm.

"So, I can either help you maintain the status quo and make sure that the attorneys are comfortable, or I can help them strengthen their sales muscles and teach them the skills that they need to increase profits."

He glared at me and hesitated momentarily. "You sold me. Go in there and do what you need to do. I trust you and your expertise."

Chapter Three

Differentiation, The Key To Standing Out From Your Competition

One of the major risks to your practice right now is not being able to define what sets you apart in a world that is cluttered, competitive, and noisy. It is becoming harder and harder to stand out and differentiate yourself. If you do not stand out, you blend in.

Many attorneys have a tough time answering these questions: How do you stand out in a sea of competition? How are you different from the last firm we retained? Why should I hire you?

Some say that what differentiates them is where they went to law school. Others say that it is how long they have been practicing. Some think that it is the prestigious firms where they have worked. All of these things help, but they are not what separates the average attorney from the rainmakers.

In this highly competitive market, it's not how good you are at what you do, it is how effective you are at marketing and selling who you are and what you do, online and offline. This statement is shocking to many attorneys. They have a hard time believing that they now have to learn the skills of networking, marketing, and selling. There is no way around this. Every practice or business prospers because someone actively and consistently works to strengthen it.

It is tempting to follow the masses, get sucked into making excuses, and believe that your practice will enhance itself. The truth is that there is no quick fix. Winning business is all about how much energy you are willing to invest to get to where you want to go. There are no shortcuts or easy routes to take to grow your practice.

You can learn the essential skills necessary to become a rainmaker as long as you are committed to doing the work that is required. Rainmakers do not wait for the phone to ring. They make their phones ring.

Many of the attorneys with whom I have worked believe that if they are good at networking, sales and profits will magically happen. Others believe that if they are good at marketing, clients and business will fall into their lap. You may be a rock star at networking and marketing, but if you are unable to convert interested prospects into clients, your practice is doomed to fail. You need a full range of skills: marketing, networking, and sales. Collectively I call this business development. Throughout this book, when I speak about client and business development, I am referring to all of the skills necessary to build your practice.

Sales are imperative to increasing profits in your practice. Every attorney knows that business development is essential for achieving revenue goals. Though client-development undertakings may look different for every attorney and every area of expertise, many attorneys are responsible for making some or all of their own opportunities.

You will likely always need to do some form of business development on a regular basis, or you won't have a practice. If you don't water your plants, they die. If you spend more than you earn, you will go broke. If you don't eat right and exercise, you will get fat. If you don't effectively and regularly sell and market your services, your practice will suffer.

Attorneys have been telling me for years that they desire to find a way to sell and market that's right for them, one that feels authentic and is comfortable to execute on a consistent basis.

I have spoken with many attorneys, and they have shared with me that they felt that selling was their greatest deficiency. When it came time to step into the initial client consultation, they did not feel comfortable in their own skin. The result of this was that they did not ask for the business and consequently did not seal the deal. It wasn't that they didn't know what to say, it was that they couldn't deliver the information in a polished, professional, and most importantly, persuasive way. These attorneys worried that they would sound pushy or come across as too sales-ish. The result was that they never attempted to step into a selling role.

But they soon realized that avoiding sales and marketing was a costly mistake and chose to get help. They built a plan that fit perfectly into their practice and made them stand out from their competition.

Once you fully understand each step in the client-development process and its purpose, you will be able to select language that fits you and your practice and then test it in the field. You will have your very own game plan.

When you have a plan, and you know how the game is played, you win. Learning the skills of the game and acquiring the right knowledge is essential to an extraordinary outcome. No matter how clever you are, if you haven't had training and you don't know the rules, the odds of succeeding are stacked against you.

Just because you've flown on an airplane doesn't mean that you could jump in the cockpit of a 747 and get the plane off the ground. You've had no formal training. Being the sales and marketing person for your practice is no different. The right knowledge and the right skills training equals exceptional results.

There is a better way and a more modern approach to achieving your goals. Your sales performance will improve immediately. Selling and marketing will become more natural, more satisfying, and more fun. You'll find that you can use these techniques and sell yourself in almost any situation.

You may be a brand-new attorney without any knowledge of the world of marketing and sales. Or you may be a seasoned attorney, using an outdated system that no longer produces results. It doesn't matter. The fact is that you now want or need a change. It's time to acquire the tools you need to purposefully and strategically drive your practice to victory.

How Do You Begin The Process Of Differentiation?

Do not turn another page until you do this exercise and give this critical aspect of your practice some consideration. Spend time thinking about what makes you different. Ask others what they think makes you stand out. Everyone has a differentiator, so don't let yourself off the hook until you discover yours.

The answer to this question will give you clarity about who you want to be in the world, who you want to be for your clients, and how you want to show up in your profession. You cannot differentiate yourself in the marketplace if you don't undertake the journey of finding out what makes you different.

Listed below are some questions to ask yourself as you go through the process:

- What is my unique offering to the marketplace?
- What are my distinct characteristics, quirks, areas of expertise, skills, and attributes?
- What is the look and feel of my brand?
- How can I integrate that uniqueness into all I do, say, write, and create?
- Once defined, how can I make it recognizable in a consistent and sustainable way?
- Can I integrate it into all of my messages, promotional materials, writings, speaking engagements, and services?
- Who is my biggest competition?
- How is what I do different from what he or she does?
- Who do I know that may give me and/or my firm an advantage in the marketplace?

Example 1: An estate planner that I once worked with sends a packet to prospective clients prior to their initial meeting. This packet includes tips, advice, resources, and the top ten questions to ask an estate-planning professional. This low-cost, high-impact packet sent a loud and clear message about how much this professional cares without ever having to say how much he cares.

Example 2: I know a divorce attorney who sends an impressive brochure to prospective clients that details vital information that one needs to know when choosing a divorce attorney. This brochure includes questions to ask and a list of referrals that may be helpful to those seeking a divorce.

Example 3: A tax attorney whom I know gifts her clients with a full car detailing service once a year. She has someone pick up the client's car from her office, take it in for detailing, and then deliver it back to her office when the client's meeting is over. A real WOW experience.

Get creative. Be adventurous. Do something that makes clients feel important and cared for. Conceive a personal and memorable experience for your clients, not just a transaction. Prospective clients will feel and know in their gut that you are distinct and that you are the best choice for them to work with.

Chapter Four
Selling is Not Advertising Or Marketing

Some attorneys have a problematic and fuzzy view of the relationship between advertising, marketing, and selling.

Marketing and advertising are everything you put *about* yourself and your practice in front of prospective clients. Selling is what turns prospects into paying clients. Selling has truly become a crusade for differentiation. It is no longer just a matter of persuasion.

If marketing and advertising guaranteed business, you wouldn't need sales skills. All you would need to do is invest a boatload of money to put yourself in front of prospective clients, and the profits would roll in. Wouldn't that be nice?

Advertising and marketing help you to command recognition about you and your practice in the marketplace. This is where the heavy lifting is done. But rarely does advertising and marketing net you any new clients. Advertising and marketing simply offer information to others about you, your firm, and the services that you provide. This recognition may lead prospective clients into your sales cycle, but it doesn't close the deal.

Advertising and marketing prime the pump. They get your sales process moving. Marketing and advertising yourself and/or your firm is a critical step toward establishing a lucrative practice.

I have known many attorneys who put thousands of dollars into marketing and advertising and not one red cent into the most critical area that helps them generate profits. Sales!

For your marketing and advertising efforts to be considered effective, someone has to actually hire you and hand you the money after a closed sale. You must sell yourself, your expertise, and the value that you bring to a client. Not hearing this, not believing this, and not doing something about it will keep your practice exactly where it is.

I recently began working with a firm that had incredible potential to flourish and appeared to be set up for an influx of new business. The attorneys in this firm did it all: networked, advertised, marketed themselves, and purchased radio spots. The phone rang, prospects wanted information, and these prospects seemed interested, and many of them even went to an initial consultation.

And yet, these meetings did not net the firm any new business. The attorneys at the firm heard lots of reasons why: *I need to think about it. Your fees seem high. I'm not sure, but I will get back to you.* Guess what? Very few people really did get back to anyone at this firm.

The one thing that the firm did not spend a penny on was teaching the attorneys how to sell their legal services. This firm spent more than $18,000 in advertising fees and in the end had nothing to show for the money spent.

The issue was that when prospective clients came in for a free consultation, the attorneys did not know the most efficient and effective way to connect with these prospects and communicate their value. They were winging their conversations and flying by the seat of their pants. Not a good long-term or solid strategy for winning business.

Together we shaped the structure, the language, the process, and the steps that the attorneys needed to take to show the prospective client the value in retaining their firm.

Many partners at firms tell me that there is no budget set aside for business-development training. Not a huge surprise. No one ever has a dedicated budget for training. Many firms choose instead to put that money into the passive part of the practice.

It is easy to produce an advertisement, talk about your services on the radio, post on social media, or do a free consultation. The hard part is doing the work to understand the sales process and what it takes for a prospect to say yes to hiring you.

Does it make sense to pour money into marketing and advertising but allot nothing for learning how to sell and seal the deal? Simply exposing your message to millions of people does not guarantee attainment of your goal. But investing in how to update your skills and evolve your sales language does. It will be the best money you ever spend on your practice. It's an investment that comes back to you in new business and increased profits.

Chapter Five
It's All In The Attitude

Becoming an unstoppable force in your practice will require you to shift your mindset and adopt a different view of the possibilities that abound in constructing a strong and gratifying practice. It's only when you think differently that you will act differently. Attitude adjustment is another class not offered in law school, or any other profession.

Your attitudes and beliefs form your thoughts and feelings, which determine your choices and decisions. Having the right attitude when you're selling is as important as any technique that you will use in business. Have you checked your attitude lately? Is yours worth emulating?

I never doubted that I had an attitude because I still hear my dad's voice saying, "You'd better watch your attitude, young lady."

Years later, I still watch my attitude, but I make sure that it's one that I'm proud to have and one that I know is contagious. I never leave home without it.

You might have top-notch legal skills, but without the right attitude you may fail to attract ideal clients and new business. Your attitudes and beliefs reside at your core. They determine how you act and react in your life and business. So take off the rose-colored glasses and take responsibility for your attitudes and beliefs. Be proud if you're that person who walks around with a good attitude and works hard to maintain it.

The attorneys who complete my training programs frequently undergo a profound shift in their attitude. A remarkable attitude is infectious.

Becoming a rainmaker requires you to be willing to try new approaches to running your practice. Becoming a rainmaker is about breaking free from old ways of thinking, doing, and being. You will soon be a positive, authoritative, and capable attorney who can not only practice law but who can sell as well.

Have you ever heard of the Law of Belief? This law states that whatever you believe, you will see. Most people have a tendency to block out any information coming in to them that is inconsistent with their beliefs. We always act in a manner that aligns with our beliefs.

Over and over attorneys say to me: *I'm not a marketer or a salesperson. I don't want people to feel like I'm selling to them. I'm not comfortable with marketing myself.* They strongly believe those statements, so they act in a way to support them. Guess what happens to their income? Not much.

When attorneys are in selling situations, they don't want to come across as selling, so they downplay or bypass the entire sales conversation. Maybe they don't ask for the business, or if they do ask, it is in a wishy-washy, weak, and passive way. They are playing the game with their negative belief system running the show. Trying to fortify a practice when you have those kinds of self-defeating thoughts generally does not work very well. Or add to the bottom line.

Change is required! Change Is Risky! Not Changing Is Even More Dangerous!

As you work your way through this book, pay attention to that voice in your head that wants you to stay away from playing a grander game. The voice that tells you that things are fine, that you don't need to focus your energy on client development. You don't need to go to another conference. You don't need to join the billions on social media. The voice that talks you out of the things that you know you need to do.

If you find yourself challenging new concepts, ideas, or strategies, try to remain open to implementing them in spite of this. Don't brush off suggestions with negative thoughts: *That won't work in my practice. Been there, done that, it didn't work for me.* A closed mind eliminates the possibility of finding solutions and new opportunities. A closed mind keeps you stagnant and ensures that you will stay right where you are. A closed mind makes achieving victory a constant battle.

You have absolutely nothing to lose and everything to gain. If your business is not where you would like it to be, why not try this out? Why limit your income and your opportunities? Why not open your life up to new possibilities and the accompanying abundance?

Chapter Six
You Are Also Selling Yourself

Regardless of whether you are in practice for yourself or you work for a large firm, clients *buy* you long before they buy your services. Always! In the business world, this is the way it is. You first, everything else after.

People want to work with and do business with people whom they like and trust. That will never change. Don't ever fool yourself into thinking that your expert legal skills will be enough. If people don't like you and trust you, they will never hire you.

Sales is still about people selling to people. Selling is about relationships. Your most effective deal-closing tool is and always will be you. And that's not going to change anytime soon. What sealed the deal back in the day is the same thing that seals the deal today. You! You are your greatest asset.

Many attorneys focus almost exclusively on selling their expertise. They pay virtually no attention to how they communicate and present *themselves.* But since your prospective clients are buying you, this makes little sense.

You are an integral part of the package. Everything you say and every move you make either pulls clients toward you or pushes them away. You either attract or repel. The way that you communicate and present yourself has a formidable effect on your credibility, your trustworthiness, and your authority.

Ask any attorney how they feel about sales and marketing, and you will likely get an unfavorable response. *I don't like selling or sales. I'm not a natural-born sales person, and I don't like to market myself. I don't have time to market my practice.* They believe these income-robbing mantras, responses, and excuses.

The result of these beliefs inevitably plays out in a predictable way. Attorneys may find themselves taking a long ride on the revenue rollercoaster. They experience highs and lows, dips and turns, and many sudden starts and stops. They will continue that ride until they change their beliefs and ultimately change their behaviors. Any negative feeling, internal conflict, or lack of confidence that they have about sales and marketing may hold them hostage and prevent them from achieving their goals for their practice. It does not have to be that way.

Sales and selling are not dirty words! For many attorneys, the concept of sales conjures up images of sleazy car salesmen, pushy telemarketers, the deluge of sales e-mails that clog our inboxes, or a slick pitch from a door-to-door solicitor.

The actions required to sell may cause attorneys anxiety, dread, or discomfort. Almost every attorney that I have ever worked with brushed off the entire notion that they have to sell. Some expressed a disgust or hatred for sales because they had a belief that selling involves manipulating people and being pushy or aggressive. They believe the notion that selling means that they have to turn into someone that they are not. Wrong!

Many outstanding attorneys use new, modern, non-sleazy methods to build their practice. Stop buying into and hanging onto that old stereotype. Conceive a new belief system.

There is absolutely nothing wrong with sales pursuits. There is only something wrong with your perception of them.

> *When you change the way you look at things, the things you look at change.*
> ~ Dr. Wayne Dyer

When you look at sales and marketing differently, things change in your practice, especially your bottom line. Every business is sustained by sales. Really, every darn one!

Selling is not about pressuring someone. It's not about manipulation. It's not about being pushy or phony. It's not about putting people in a head-lock until they say yes. Keeping that negative mindset diminishes your clout.

Selling is about helping people get what they need. Selling is about leading and moving people to action. You are the facilitator of that transaction. When others take action, you are compensated. Selling is about exchanging your expertise for money.

This is no different than an architect drawing up plans for a new home, a surgeon repairing a torn ligament, or a mechanic putting in a new transmission. Services are rendered and money is exchanged. It is a simple, straightforward transaction.

What Signals Are You Broadcasting To Potential Clients?

You get back what you put out. The problem is that most of the time attorneys aren't conscious of the signals that they're giving off, that they are not comfortable with the client conversation or not confident in promoting and selling their services. Whatever the case, it shows.

It doesn't matter how hard you work, and it doesn't matter how good you are as an attorney. If you convey a low level of certainty to prospective clients, you will not attract the clients that your practice needs to survive.

Self-assured attorneys have the ability to broadcast that self-assurance, a quality that draws clients and opportunities to them. They are poised in almost all circumstances. This does not translate to cocky, phony, or aggressive.

Angela, a divorce attorney with whom I recently worked, was a caring, kind, and influential woman. Angela contacted me because she was losing business on a level that concerned her. She thought that if someone coached her in a better communication style, that would turn things around. For years she had worked solely on referrals and did not need to put much effort into business development. Life was good for Angela. But now she was confused and needed my help.

She told me that no matter what she did or said during her initial meetings, luncheons, and networking events, people never called her back or hired her. The only way for me to gauge where the problem was was to witness what she was doing when she interacted with people in a real situation. I joined her for an event sponsored by an organization to which we both belonged. It took me less than five minutes to see what was causing her to lose business and causing people to want to forget that they had ever met her.

Angela was kind and warm, but when she networked, she became a steamroller who forced herself and her cards on people who didn't ask for them. She looked like a Las Vegas blackjack dealer. She walked up to a table where eight businesswomen were talking and leaned into a space between two of them and dealt her cards in Vegas-dealer style. She uttered a few words to them and proceeded to the next table.

What Angela didn't see, but I did, was the look of shock on the women's faces. I had viewed the train wreck that she left at each table, a terrible first and lasting impression.

No one felt sociable or cordial toward Angela because she was on a mission to pass out as many cards as she could in one hour, not have a few conversations that could lead to business. She clearly showed that she had no interest in getting to know anyone, she simply wanted to pass out cards.

When Angela's practice began to get tough as the economy worsened, Angela turned up the heat on her networking efforts. She turned it up so high that people around her felt burned, not welcome. She was acting desperate. Her approach was not attracting business, it was repelling business. She had developed a bad reputation that almost destroyed her practice.

Angela needed a little sales coaching, but what she needed more from me was communication coaching. Angela took a few months off from networking. We worked together on a new approach that was softer, more inviting, and focused on engaging others. Her business is back on track, and she is a more pleasant attorney. She no longer wears that business-killing scent of desperation.

Pay attention to what you project to your clients and how they perceive you.

Chapter Seven

Getting Real Is The Path To Getting Real Results

Taking an assessment of your current practice may lead to the disappointing discovery that you're not even close to where you want to be. This may hurt a bit, but recognizing the reality of your situation is essential to your success. Doing nothing is no longer an option if you don't want to stay where you are. Taking action achieves results.

Do not underestimate the value of making a brutally honest and accurate assessment of your practice. You can't begin to move and grow your practice until you face reality. Avoiding self-assessment is a dangerous form of denial that leads to unwise and costly mistakes on your path to prosperity. A booming practice must be built on a strong foundation. Denying any part of your present situation weakens that foundation.

The truth hurts, but you can't move forward without first facing the facts. Don't treat your practice like a messy garage. When you open the door, you may see a mess, but shutting the door doesn't mean that the mess is gone. The same is true for your practice. You can't keep pretending that you have the consummate practice when you know that there is a mess waiting for you each day when you go to the office. Take a hard look at what is working and what is not working.

Because time, energy, and money are limited, identifying priorities and taking the appropriate actions is an important step toward fulfillment for any professional. An attorney who expends time on the wrong tasks will fail to make much rain. An example of this is focusing on designing a perfect website rather than spending time on client development.

Do not create a diversion around what actually needs to be done. Stop participating in activities that only look like they move the needle of your practice. Instead, get clear on the actions that really do move the needle.

Reality may sting, but denial is worse and much more agonizing. Reality is truth, and when you know the truth, you can do something about it. Many attorneys don't want to look at what is because it isn't what they want. If you want more, you have to do more. Discovering that you aren't where you want to be should be liberating. It puts you on the path to where you want to go.

You have two choices in any given moment: action or inaction. I'm not talking about the kind of action that you take only when you feel like it or when it's convenient. I am talking about the kind of action that requires digging in and working hard to produce results. Small daily steps yield huge results. We all always have two alternatives, do something or do nothing.

Taking action, sometimes significant action, is the only way to construct change. Many attorneys go to excessive lengths to escape change, even when that change will produce a number of benefits and measurable results.

Why do so many brilliant attorneys find dreary revenues and unfulfilled expectations acceptable? Why do they complain and carry on about how dreadful their practice is, yet they are unwilling to do anything about it? Why would an intelligent attorney keep doing what he is doing if it's not working? Does he believe that change is so scary that he'd rather be miserable than risk the unknown? No change equals no growth. No growth equals no practice.

We all like a sense of safety and security in our lives. Some of us need more security than others. But the need for security may prevent us from taking calculated risks and may make us steer clear of anything that resembles change. Fear of change may rob us of our potential and steal our possibilities.

Don't stagnate in the comfort zone. You have a choice. You have the ability to make bold changes, and every change makes a difference in your life and your business.

For example, you could pick up the phone (not send an e-mail) and re-connect with past clients, take a prospect out to coffee or lunch, make an appearance at networking events where your perfect clients network, attend a luncheon once or twice a month, write an article and post it to a blog, or learn how to use LinkedIn and try your hand at social media. Get moving!

Chapter Eight

The Gap Between Knowing And Doing

Do you know what you need to do but don't do it? Knowing does not equal doing. Most people know how important exercise and proper nutrition are but don't work out or eat well. Attorneys understand what could be done to forge new opportunities, yet they do not do it. Knowing what to do and how to do it isn't enough to ensure a favorable long-term outcome.

For example, an attorney might understand that writing articles and contributing to industry journals are a perfect way to showcase her expertise, but she doesn't devote time to writing. An attorney could be aware that networking luncheons are a terrific way to be seen, and somehow these luncheons never make it onto his calendar. Some attorneys know that they should attend industry conferences to make more connections, but they never take the time to do the research to find out which ones are a good fit for their practice.

It is time to move the knowledge out of your head and put it into action. The delay in the transfer of knowledge to action today is mind-boggling.

There is a tremendous gap today between knowing and doing. You are in complete control of closing that gap. Most people know so much more than they think they do. They over-know and under-do. How wide is that gap in your practice? How much of a gap can you and your practice realistically sustain?

Knowledge doesn't produce results, action does. I hear attorneys say, *I know what I need to do. I know the actions that I need to take.* Knowing is only half of the equation. The other half is doing, and doing it again and again until you develop the self-discipline to get the results that you want, and until the process becomes a habit. You can't dabble in self-discipline and expect to prosper. Combining knowledge and action leads to results.

It is ridiculous to think that you could go to the gym once or twice a year and suddenly become a fitness guru; buy a cookbook, prepare a few meals, and become a master chef; or hit a bucket of golf balls on the driving range and become a golf pro. Self-discipline is needed to improve almost anything. Do you want to lose weight? Do you want to learn a foreign language? Do you want to improve your sales results? Self-discipline is the speediest, most effective, and longest-lasting method that you may take to reach your goal.

Do you cringe at the idea of repeating an activity that you find difficult or doing a task over and over again in order to perfect it? Developing a skill that doesn't come naturally to you may feel like a daunting task. You start the process but, inevitably, never see it through to completion because of a lack of self-discipline. The task may have become too difficult, so you give up. When you lack self-discipline, it's easier to give up than to push through to the other side.

Discipline drives your actions, attitudes, behaviors, and outcomes. When you lack discipline and don't have a clear understanding of what you want, why you want it, and how to get it, you will be met with a series of setbacks and disappointments. Your life will be filled with frustration, anxiety, and failure. It doesn't have to be that way.

After a few bad meetings with potential clients, a few presentations that yield no new business, or a dozen phone calls to prospects that go nowhere, you might decide that you don't have what it takes to be phenomenal at sales.

Really, are you giving up that easily? Do you think that all it takes to be good at something is to try it a couple of times? You don't have to love the task, but you do have to hunker down and finish it if you want to grow your business. I don't love accounting, but I know that I have to keep my records up-to-date if I want to keep my finances in order.

Do you think that top athletes love to leap out of bed at 5:00 on cold winter mornings and put their bodies through hours of arduous training? They know that to win they must be disciplined in all of the areas of their lives that affect their performance.

A study many years back reported that the majority of people want to be happy, healthy, thin, and rich. No surprise there. Some are willing to pay the price, but many want something for nothing. Perfectly crafted excuses wait in the wings about why they can't be wealthy, happy, healthy, and fit and why they lack the self-discipline needed to do everything in their control to achieve their goals.

Everyone knows that we all should exercise, eat right, and get plenty of sleep, but the price may be too high, and sometimes the motivation is too low to do what we ought to do. Everyone knows how to save money, but the immediate pleasure of treating ourselves to something that we can't afford is much more exciting. The only way to be happy, healthy, thin, and rich is to pay the price, do the work, and remain self-disciplined.

If you want to flourish as an attorney, self-discipline is crucial. You need to learn the necessary skills and then refine them. You may experience a few failures along the way as you work on improving a skill, but eventually you will conquer every new skill. Try tasks that are outside your comfort zone, and perfect them until the new task becomes easy and comfortable.

I said earlier that we all know what self-discipline is and how it may be achieved, but knowing something doesn't ensure that we will do it.

With respect to saving money or losing weight, you know what must be done. It will never change. Eat less and move more. Save more and spend less. If everyone knows this, why are so many people unable to lose weight or grow their bank account?

Knowing isn't doing. Knowing isn't enough to produce results. Combine the knowing and the doing, and you get results.

Chapter Nine
Are You Making Rain Or Making Excuses?

Excuses! Excuses! What would people do without their excuses? Excuses are pesky, self-destructive things that help people to avoid responsibility. Today, the ability to focus on the task at hand is seriously underrated.

How many times have you made an excuse? *I don't have time. I don't know how. I'm too busy. I'm not good at that. I don't have time to go to networking events. I'm too busy for marketing activities.* Making excuses is common. Believing them is terminal.

It's rare when people accept the challenge. People who have the rainmaking mindset say, *Even though I'm busy, I will make time for marketing this week. I will work a few extra hours and network on LinkedIn. I will attend a bar association lunch meeting, even though my schedule is tight.*

People would rather resort to making excuses. Sure, things happen, and at times you may get busy and get pulled off of your business-development plan, but making business development a priority is important to your success.

Tally Up The Cost

Making excuses costs you plenty! Serious dollars are at stake when you make excuses. Making excuses means that your money-making ability may come to a halt. Try putting a dollar amount on how much money you're losing in your business when you make excuses.

Excuse-making is becoming the norm, and it's a whopping reason why so many practices fail. Chronic excuse-making is a way to evade the necessity of doing the hard work. The only cure for this chronic condition is action. Sharp attorneys know that if debilitating excuse-making is not cured, their practice may be crushed.

Ultimately, you are the only thing that you can control. Pay attention to how often you catch yourself making excuses. Excuses fuel failure. Remember that every time you rattle off an excuse, it's like pressing down hard on the brakes of your practice.

The life and the business that you make for yourself are shaped through your actions or your excuses. We become a mirror image of them. Your actions either catapult you forward or hurl you backwards. When things are moving in the wrong direction, be mindful of this, and reverse the trend. Adjust your thinking and your actions to get back on track. If you're marching in the right direction, you are moving closer to achieving your goals. If you're trudging in the wrong direction, you are moving farther away from achievement.

The bottom line is that we make up excuses to justify why we're not doing what we know we should do. Attorneys occasionally tell themselves white lies to avoid the pain of reality. However, refusing to face the facts may have real consequences.

It is time to enter the no-excuse zone! Stop making excuses and start making rain.

You Can Build Your Practice While Billing Time

Many attorneys have shared with me the frustration of the cycle that plays out over and over in their practice. Their business-development efforts produce leads, which effect results in the form of business. Then they devote their time to client work. While they are focused on client work, they dial down their momentum in relation to networking, marketing, and sales, only to find themselves finishing up with one client with no prospects or new clients on the horizon. The wild ride on the revenue roller coaster has begun. They have the daunting task of starting the process of making rain all over again.

I frequently hear, *I'm too busy to do any marketing right now. I can't take the time for networking or sales. I need to focus on billing. The time that I spend selling is not billable time.* This distasteful ritual may be averted.

Many professionals with whom I work come up with the same excuses. It does not matter the profession, you still need to keep up the pursuit and make time to keep your client pipeline full.

When you begin to command and demand more of yourself, triumph will follow. When you find the strength from within to take full responsibility for your life and your potential, your prominence is realized. You have the muscle to raise the bar on yourself and set higher standards.

Balancing Prospecting And Billable Time

We all have exactly twenty-four hours in each day, and perhaps only one or two of these hours are available for business development. By now you are mindful that every attorney knows that steady prospecting is essential for achieving revenue goals. They also know that they are responsible for their own livelihood. So why do so many attorneys struggle with sporadic and ineffective prospecting efforts?

It comes down to not knowing exactly how to efficiently and effectively utilize their precious hours for prospecting. They have not dialed into a plan and a process that they can live with.

The rainmakers whom I know organize their day into specific time blocks dedicated to each activity necessary to conduct their business, concentrating their focus and eliminating distractions. They develop a process and a plan to get the most out of every day.

They are flexible and resourceful in their quest to maximize time for sales and marketing activities, and they minimize distractions that steal their billable time.

I will not go into the thousands of time-management tools available to you. I would suggest that you research the possibilities and find one that works best for you. Some rainmakers use old-fashioned paper calendars, and others use online technology. You may wish to determine what your preference is.

My goal is to help you gain awareness around how critical time-management is to your success and income and help you shift your mindset about how you schedule and manage time for prospecting and other client-development activities. Take an honest look at the consequences of the choices that you are making about where and how to spend your time.

The evidence does not lie. You are either making superb use of your time, or you are squandering time on activities that do not generate income.

Chapter Ten

Standing Out And Being Unforgettable

It is much easier to make a terrific first impression than it is to change a negative one. When you meet people for the first time, they form opinions about you. It's human nature. Within seconds of meeting someone for the first time, your appearance, body language, and nonverbal communication together make a first impression.

The mastery of a positive first impression cannot be overstated. First impressions are lasting impressions. People make assumptions and think that they know everything about you in the brief initial time spent with you.

Make a good first impression, and the relationship will evolve from there. Make a bad first impression, and your relationship may always be an uphill battle. A bad first impression may also mean that you might never get another chance.

In a perfect world, friendships, relationships, and business contacts would all develop naturally and blossom exactly how you'd like, but that's not the world we live in. Every time you meet someone, you make an impression. Whether you make a good impression or bad impression is up to you.

When you first meet someone, they will naturally form an opinion about you based upon how you look, what you say, and how you present yourself. The way that you enter a room, the way that you communicate, and the way that you move speaks volumes about you.

These opinions may be the basis for many important decisions that someone else makes about you. Others hastily assess if they can see themselves doing business with you and if you are a good fit for them. This is why it is essential to know how to make a superb first impression when meeting new people, one that will help you achieve the happiness that you desire.

How Do You Respond When Asked What You Do?

Regardless of whether you are at a business event, a one-on-one meeting, socializing at a party, or playing a round of golf, you need to be ready to deliver your fifteen-second commercial, also known as your personal introduction.

It's the fifteen-second answer to the question, *what do you do?* The thirty-second commercial has been replaced with a fifteen-second commercial, thanks to the attention span of most people, which is shrinking at this moment.

Your commercial is a short description of your practice and who you are, which enables others to understand your area of expertise, they type of clients you work with, and what value you bring to the relationship. Your commercial should sound conversational and natural. You want to appear composed, enthusiastic, and professional. Make it memorable, not outrageous.

You are competing with many other attorneys. Your commercial should allow you to stand out from the crowd. Whether it is the vocabulary you choose or a specific achievement you mention, you want to engage the listener and give them an opportunity to see your personality shine through. What you say and how you say it either attracts business to you or repels it away from you.

The success of your commercial depends on your ability to craft a message that offers a strong promise of benefits to your target market. A good personal introduction immediately differentiates you from your competitors and makes you unforgettable.

What do you do? is the most common questic meeting someone for the first time. If what you say and interesting, you'll be remembered. If what you say is uninteresting, you'll be forgotten on the spot.

I attend many networking and business events every month, and I hear hundreds of commercials. I can always spot the practiced and polished professional who put time and energy into her commercial. It's timed, it's planned, and it doesn't sound canned. It's concise and descriptive, not long and scattered. It's delivered with passion and confidence instead of fear and anxiety. The best commercials stand out and are remembered.

Treat your fifteen-second commercial like a Super Bowl ad. Make it short, and make it memorable. Act like you are getting paid for the opportunity to recite it. Compose a commercial that doesn't sound like that of everyone else.

A good commercial may help you entice new clients, get referrals, and make yourself memorable. A bad one nets you nothing and may make a negative impression that might never go away.

When someone asks you what you do, your answer to the question should not be about you. Many attorneys make the mistake of answering the question with a statement about themselves. Try this instead:

Example 1: Hello, I'm Marsha Walker, a divorce attorney and conflict resolution expert. I represent individuals going through a divorce who want to shield their children from the trauma that a divorce can cause. I focus on trying to stay out of the court system and attempting to resolve issues civilly so that divorcing couples may move on with their lives as amicably as possible.

Example 2: I am Stan Sanders, a business attorney. I represent a wide range of clients, from construction companies to those involved in real estate. I specialize in providing superior resolution of simple and common issues to the most complex of conflicts and do this in the most efficient and cost-effective manner possible.

Is your commercial a clear, concise, and fascinating fifteen seconds? Or is it a two-minute ramble that engenders confusion in your listener? Do you even know? There may be some anxiety associated with a personal introduction if you aren't used to delivering one or if you're uneasy when it comes to talking about yourself or your business.

Most people think that they need to tell prospects everything that they have to offer, but this is not the case. Your commercial is just a snapshot of what you do and how you help. Focus on the results that you provide, and make your personal introduction about the listener, not about you. If someone wants to know more, they will ask. Make your introduction short and sweet instead of long and boring. Never underestimate the influence of a good commercial.

Whether you're experienced or new to networking, you must proudly own your commercial, or you will blow your chance at making a good first impression. The attorneys who get in the door are the ones who swiftly and strongly communicate their value. Your commercial needs to hit the mark, or you're going to lose revenue and referral opportunities.

Continually perfecting and practicing your commercial ensures that you are always able to put your best foot forward as your business grows and changes and your client base expands.

Keep it simple, make it memorable, and clearly tell people what you do and how you can help them or others. It's important to focus your message on the clients with whom you work and how you work with them, not on how incredible you are, the wonderful things you do, and how long you have been in business. This is not your time to brag. Take control of your commercial, and you will create more opportunities and close more sales.

The next time that someone walks up to you, shakes your hand, and asks what you do, say it loud, say it proud, and recite your commercial with authority.

Five More Ways To Be Unforgettable

1. **Start with a genuine compliment.** Giving someone a compliment is always the most genuine way to engage them. When you compliment someone, their usual response is to smile and thank you, and likely they will ask you something about yourself.

You have now engaged this person, and they have let their guard down. They feel like they can trust you.

2. **Be a master at listening.** Only when you listen to people do you find out what their needs are, and then you can figure out if you have a solution for them or if you should refer them to someone else who more closely fits their needs. It is impossible to listen and talk at the same time. Be known for being a listener rather than a talker. Be interested, not interesting. That means talking less and listening more.

3. **Look people in the eyes.** Give someone you meet your full attention. Don't look around the room for the next prospect. Don't text, check your e-mail, or respond to a call in the middle of a conversation. You will never recover from that rude business blunder.

4. **Give to get.** Think of something that you can give to someone rather than something that you can get. Offer to send them information about a topic of interest to them, or connect them with a contact that you think they should know.

5. **Be a resource.** Listen to someone's problems, what causes them stress and sleepless nights. Then you can be the one to offer a solution. Not every person will be your ideal client, but someone to whom you offer your help will be grateful, and they will remember you as a knowledgeable, positive resource.

Make your first impressions count, and never underestimate the importance of others. If the new people that you meet remember you in a positive way, you position yourself for even more abundant business opportunities down the road.

Chapter Eleven

Using A Process Translates To Profits

If I told you that there was something that you could do right now in your practice that would make you more money, would you do it? Of course you would! If this tool is so mighty and yields such immense results, why isn't everyone using it? Because it takes commitment, discipline, and practice to use it properly and make it work.

The tool is called a sales process. If you don't have one, you need to get one. If you do have a process but reject using it, it's time to wipe away the cob webs and blow off the dust because it's required on the path to a flourishing practice.

What Is A Business-Development (Or Sales) Process?

The textbook definition of a business-development process is a structured, systematic, logical, and documented step-by-step approach to selling a product or service where a progression of defined steps is followed and results in the completion of a sale. My modified definition of this process is when someone uses a set of structured and defined steps that effectively move an interested client into an invested client and a raving fan. It's a process and a map that efficiently guides you to developing relationships and keeping clients.

A sales process is not robotic, inflexible, artificial, or inauthentic. If you're feeling opposition toward this dynamic tool, this chapter is for you. Please remain open to the information here. Don't underestimate the vitality hidden in this tool until you fully understand the impact that it will have on your practice.

Using a sales process offers you the best outcome in closing sales. If a process is based on maximizing the probability of closing, reducing the sales cycle, and increasing profitability, it's foolish for anyone not to use a process. If the process is the road map that facilitates your ability to close more sales in a shorter period of time, all attorneys should clamor to use this tool.

The sales process maximizes productivity and results for anyone that uses one. Again, don't discount the advantages that are part and parcel of this tool. It is a must-have in your firm's tool box.

Many attorneys refuse to use a process, to follow a step-by-step approach that produces results, because they would rather be right and stay stuck where they are than do what is necessary to build a profitable practice. They would rather go with the flow, take a chance, and let the business happen naturally versus ensuring that it goes according to their plan.

Those who don't use a sales process are using the ineffective *winging it* process. Their process is not structured or logical, it's scattered and inefficient and produces poor results. Or they have one or two skills in their tool box and get lucky every now and then.

Mastering one or two skills alone won't generate the same results as understanding and mastering the entire process. There are parts and pieces to every process, and some of them are special for every attorney. But the capacity of the tool is not fully realized until you use all of the parts and pieces together. Understanding and applying the principles of the entire process leaves nothing to chance.

Everything is a process. Every sale involves a process of defined steps, and skipping a step or going out of order typically results in a lost sale. A recipe is a process. It tells you, step-by-step, what you need to do to get a certain outcome. If you are baking a soufflé, a recipe takes you from start to finish, covering all the steps in between. A business-development process takes you from attracting a prospect to closing the business, covering all of the steps along the way.

The word process comes from the Latin word procedure, which means to proceed, and is a series of operations or stages that lead to a specific outcome. Regardless of what you sell, the process is like a production line, and it must follow a certain sequence.

Neglecting to use a structured process will guarantee that your efforts will be a colossal waste of precious time, money, and energy. Every fruitful sale is the result of a series of consistent behaviors and actions. Using these behaviors and actions constitutes a strategic business decision.

Trust the process. Attorneys who use a structured process stop relying on luck, chance, wishing, hoping, and praying when selling. They use and trust the process because it works. Many attorneys soon realize that using a process makes sense, and they hope that their competition doesn't know about it. And they see that it is logical and wonder why everyone isn't doing it.

When you use a process, you maintain better relationships and bolster your business more strategically. If you're chasing potential clients, they're not calling you back. If you make excuses, your process may be broken. If your potential clients won't communicate with you, your process may be nonexistent. You simply can't afford to not invest your time in learning to use this supreme tool.

There are many moving parts to the process: building chemistry and a connection, encouraging trust, asking impactful questions, talking about fees and budgets, handling objections, securing the business, and closing the sale.

Keep in mind that every business is different, and every practice has a different process. One size does not fit all. You need a custom process to ensure the potency and efficiency of your practice. Designing sales processes is one of my favorite things to do for attorneys because there is a vast amount of energy, results, and impact inherent in this task.

When attorneys use a process, they see both their profits and their performance soar. Top performers have a process for generating good leads from multiple sources. They have an intake system for categorizing leads, managing them, organizing them, and following up on them. Everything attorneys do is semi-scripted, rehearsed, fine-tuned, and memorized. They are consistent in their efforts, and their efforts yield terrific results every time.

The Seven-Step Sales Process

The following step-by-step approach shows you how to allow a conversation with a prospective client to happen naturally. Each step forges a stronger case for your service and expertise without hard selling and leads to a more influential, stress-free close.

Even though the conversation is loosely structured, it permits an intuitive, authentic, and natural conversational flow. Please know that there are many other nuances to a sales process. I customize the process to each client based upon their personality, practice, and style, and below I have given you a framework for you to use so that you may begin to customize your own process.

Step 1: Connect, Open, And Build Genuine Rapport

Your goal is to establish trust by connecting with your client. Ask questions. Get in her world. Forgo the temptation to talk about yourself and go into monologue mode. Find commonalities that help you break the ice. Discover mutual interests. Use your imagination, and make it about her.

Step 2: Needs Analysis

It is here that you must ask questions, uncover needs, and find out what is going on in a prospect's world. This is not the time to launch into an extensive description about your services and how long you've been practicing law. This is precisely where most prospective clients will tune out and wonder why you are talking about yourself and not focusing on their issues.

This step is about strengthening credibility, not by talking about yourself and what you offer but by demonstrating your listening skills and your business approach. The spotlight should shine on the prospective client.

Step 3: Ask The Prospect To Share With You

Get permission to get personal about what is going on in someone's life. Let him know that you're going to ask questions so that you can better understand his needs and what solution will be most helpful to him. Tell him that the only way to see if you are a good fit is to dive into the details of his pain, his issues, and his problems. You want to make sure that you understand the key factors driving his decision to seek your counsel.

Step 4: Ask Questions And Listen

Here is where some attorneys miss the mark. They're so concerned about what to say and how to say it that they either don't ask enough questions or they don't dig deep enough. When you ask intelligent and purposeful questions, you swiftly leap from attorney to a trusted resource and expert in the client's eyes. They understand that you know what you're doing and that you're there to listen to and help them.

One of the most important questions to ask is what goals the prospective client would like to achieve if they work with you. This will give you immense insight into the way that it is best for you to present your services as solutions to their problems.

Step 5: Summarize And Prioritize

Make sure that you communicate effectively. Summarize what the client has shared with you so that she knows that you understand her situation. The summary takes thirty to sixty seconds and will ensure that you and your client are both moving in the same direction. Clients appreciate when you paraphrase what they've said to you because it proves to them that you were engaged and paying attention. Use their exact words and language. This step further increases your credibility and value and gets the client geared up to talk about solutions.

Step 6: Collaborate To Find Solutions

You've assessed the opportunity, and now it's time to discuss options and solutions. Instead of launching into selling mode, here is your chance to mention a few of the services that you offer before you present an official proposal. Instead of making a number of suggestions, ask questions so that you may hone in and find the right solution together. Brainstorm. This engages the client and allows him to discover what it is that he really needs and that you're the person to provide it.

Step 7: The Commitment

Assume that a decision has not been made and that the sale has not closed. Don't skip this step. This is where everything could fall apart. Set up the next meeting or call by deciding on a specific time and date. This ensures that you leave every meeting knowing exactly what will happen next. Never depart without knowing what the next step will be for all parties involved.

Using a process gives you definable steps, predictable outcomes, and measurable results.

Chapter Twelve
Nonverbal Communication: What Is Your Body Saying?

The first moments of meeting someone have a huge impact on whether they will hire you. Your verbal communication is important, but your non-verbal communication is just as critical. This cannot be overlooked or ignored.

Nonverbal communication refers to the communication that occurs without using spoken language. Nonverbal communication, often otherwise known as body language, is important in getting prospective clients to listen to your recommendations and hire you.

The message that you convey in your client conversations consists of 55 percent nonverbal communication, 38 percent tone of voice, and only 7 percent in the words that you use.

There are two levels of communication. One is conscious communication. This includes words, writing, actions, and body movements. The other is subconscious communication, which includes the feelings, or the signals, that you're sending out to the person with whom you are communicating.

We all know and have had those feelings. At some point you may have thought, *I'm feeling a good vibe. I've got a good feeling about this. I don't have a good feeling about this person. This situation makes me uneasy.*

We are constantly sending out vibes and signals. When you're talking to people and meeting prospects, you can say and do all the right things, but if you feel something else on a subconscious level, none of the things you say or do will matter to your client. The reason for this is because as the old saying goes, *it's not what you say, it's how you say it.*

The feelings that you have beneath the surface are infused into how you say something. Believe it or not, the person that you're talking to can feel this. People will use their gut, their intuition to make a decision, and much of that intuition is governed by what you convey with your subconscious communication. Don't underestimate the importance of this.

In any situation, the impression that you make when first meeting someone will define the nature of the relationship. Not only is this true in your personal life, it is true in business as well. **Example:** You might verbally communicate, *I am sure that this solution will fit your needs*, but your body language conveys, *I know that I can't pull this off.* Your words do not match what your body is saying. There is a disconnect, and people feel it.

Many times others don't know exactly what they feel or can't tell you why they feel weird about you. They only know on a subconscious level that what you say and what your body language conveys is incongruent.

If you go into a consultation with your focus on the close, your mindset is on signing the paperwork, and your intention is to land a new client and seal the deal. The prospective client senses this. When your energy and focus is on the end of the meeting, you are putting out vibes that you're there for the sale and nothing else.

When a potential client senses that you're starting the conversation with the goal of sealing the deal and that your questions are centered around your agenda and not her needs, concerns, and problems, her guard goes up. She plays her cards close to the vest, she withholds information, and she won't be completely truthful. She can't! She is playing it safe.

Imagine that during an initial consultation with a prospective client, you get the feeling that the meeting is going well, you think that you have a good connection, and you sense that the conversation is moving along fine. You may even be thinking that you landed a new client or feel certain that you will close the sale.

But the opposite is actually true. You totally misread the situation. Your prospect can't wait to tell you that he needs to think about it, because when you first began the meeting, he saw you as someone with a personal agenda and an intention that was focused on you, not on him.

The signals that you sent out said that you were only interested in the sale. People are intelligent and can spot and sense your agenda in short order. This prospect concluded that you were not the type of person that he wanted to do business with, and the sale was lost in the first few minutes. It's a scenario that plays itself out over and over, and there is only one reason why. You're making it about you and not about the client.

Attorneys who do a poor job of reading their clients may be unaware of how their body language contradicts their spoken words, since the awareness of one's body language depends on the objective feedback of others. What is your body language conveying?

Chapter Thirteen
People Buy Emotionally, Then Justify Logically

It's no secret that people (yes, you too) buy based on emotion and then justify their purchases later with facts and logic. Regardless of what you sell, whether it is a product, a service, or advice, people buy based on feelings. No matter how much we think that people are rational beings who occasionally act emotionally, the reality is that they are emotional beings who occasionally act rationally.

Buying decisions are always the result of a change in the customer's emotional state. While information helps to change that emotional state, it's the emotion that's important, not the information. Never underestimate the importance and power of emotions. Feelings are the fuel that prompt people to hire you.

Logic makes people think. Emotions make people act. Put another way, logic makes people need to think about it. Emotion makes people ready to hire you. It's up to you to take them from logic to emotion.

With the exception of necessities such as gas and groceries, almost everything that people buy, they buy on emotion. Sure, logic is and always will be a small part of a buying decision, but a decision to buy is primarily driven by emotion.

Since nothing about buying behavior is logical, you can't use logic to sell. Think of a situation where you had bulletproof facts, reason, and logic on your side and believed that there was absolutely no way that the other person could say no to your perfectly constructed argument. To do so would be impossible because there was no other logical solution or answer.

And then the other person dug in his heels and refused to budge. He was not at all persuaded by your logic. Were you stunned?

This happens every day in the dance of buying and selling. Attorneys sit down at the table to hammer out the details of a deal, armed with facts, attempting to use logic to influence the other party. They figure that by piling on the data and using reason to explain their side of the situation, they can construct a solution that is simply irrefutable and get the other party to say yes.

This is a recipe for disaster because decision-making isn't logical, it's emotional. You must take the time to tune in and turn on the emotions in your prospect.

Attorneys who don't enjoy feeling their own emotions will never touch their clients' emotions. But a keen attorney knows that people buy emotionally, and they are willing to go there with a prospective client. Emotion is what drives a prospect's buying decision. Emotion trumps logic every time!

Some attorneys will argue this point to death because they're uncomfortable with the notion that in order to sell, they must access prospects' emotions. Like it or not, that's the way it is. It's reality. Arguing with reality prevents attorneys from earning a considerable living.

You may be thinking, *Emotions, I don't do emotions. Feelings, yuk, I stopped feeling in the 1970s. That's too touchy-feely for me.* When I hear an attorney say that he is uncomfortable with feelings and emotions, I know that what he is really saying is, *I'm not comfortable with my own feelings and emotions, I sure as heck don't want to deal with someone else's.* Keep in mind that selling is not about you and how you feel. It is about how your prospect feels.

If you don't like the word emotion, replace it with chemistry. If you do not develop chemistry with your prospective client, there likely will be no sale and no new business.

Feeling that chemistry is critical in your prospect's decision-making process. Some people are naturals at effortlessly putting people at ease. They have an innate ability to detect authentic chemistry and get people to open up and feel comfortable with them. Others are not so lucky and have to work at it.

By now, you should know if you connect with people easily or if it takes you a bit more time. Either way is okay. Just make sure that you get this concept.

Still not convinced? Are clients and opportunities disappearing before your eyes? You know what I mean. The ones that you thought were guaranteed to hire you or choose your firm but that slipped through your fingers at the last second. Or you found yourself working diligently on a promising opportunity when suddenly, with no explanation, the opportunity spins out of control and is lost?

You're certain that you have connected with, communicated with, and engaged the prospect. You clarified everything that your prospect needed to know about your service, and they have a sufficient budget. You tell yourself that it's in the bag and start high-fiving yourself in your mind.

Then out of nowhere you hear something like: *We're very impressed and will give it some thought! Your presentation was incredible. We'll keep you in the loop. What you say makes a lot of sense. Let me run it by the others. I need to think about it, and I'll get back to you.*

Why does this happen? You were likely attempting to motivate and inspire someone to buy from you using logic, not emotion.

You may be the best and brightest attorney in the world. You may make every rational argument to demonstrate why it makes sense for someone to do business with you, but if you don't appeal to your prospects on an emotional level, you're just another person trying to sell them something.

You are missing a big part of what influences their buying decision. Emotion!

The swiftest way to interest more clients, grow your practice, and significantly increase your bottom line is to purposefully take your clients on the journey from logic to emotion.

Chapter Fourteen

Effective Initial Consultations ~ Making The Most Of The First Five Minutes

Opening is the new closing. The opening is the most critical and the least forgiving part of any meeting. The consequences of a bad start or a misstep may result in a closed door and lost business. When an attorney shows up to a meeting with the mindset of sealing the deal and closing the sale, the energy shifts, the intention is wrong, and the prospect knows it.

Attorneys shoot themselves in the foot and use what little time they have to connect and engage by talking about themselves and their accomplishments. That sets the wrong tone, the prospect's guard goes up, and the campaign to win new business begins anew. If you are trying to forge a partnership or a relationship, act like a partner, not an attorney who has the sole intention of making another sale.

If your intention is aligned with your client's needs and wants, you will look, sound, and feel much different than anyone else that she talks to. Your client's negative perception of attorneys may be based upon her past experience. Over time prospective clients form a defense system to protect themselves, which comes from previous experience.

If a prospective client has in her mind that all attorneys are arrogant or full of themselves and you show up talking about yourself, your accomplishments, your education, and your clientele, her feelings will be confirmed.

If she is in the same frame of mind and you ask questions about her, get into her world, find out who she is, and are open and warm, you will contradict that frame of mind.

I see this happen every day when I am assessing and observing initial meetings in role play or improv situations. Many attorneys lose opportunities by acting in the first five minutes as if the meeting is about them rather than about the client. They feel obliged to demonstrate how clever and experienced they are by telling stories about themselves as the client tries to discuss his situation.

This is not the time to put the spotlight on you. Shine it on him. Plus, it is way too early in the conversation for the prospect to hear and absorb your monologue. Why? He is too busy getting a handle on how he feels in your presence and is deciding if you are even worth listening to.

I hate to be the bearer of bad news, but prospects don't care about you. They don't care about where you went to school. They don't care about who you've worked with in the past. They care about themselves and their situation. They care about results. You can talk about yourself later. You should not put yourself at center stage at the beginning of a meeting.

Prospects watch every move you make and listen to every word you say.

The two most critical elements in forming profitable client relationships are emotional involvement and trust. Without emotion, people will not act on your recommendations. Without trust, people will not believe that you are acting in their best interests.

It's much easier to make a positive first impression than to change a negative one. When you meet prospects for the first time, they form opinions about you, and you soon become positioned in their minds either as a typical pompous attorney or as a trusted advisor.

The first five minutes will make or break what happens next. When you conduct meaningful initial consultations in which you discuss your prospect's needs and problems, she becomes emotionally involved. You show her that you understand her on a level that very few attorneys do, and you can dramatically shorten the time that it takes to gain her trust.

The greatest impact that you can have on the outcome of a deal happens at the beginning of the conversation, not the end. The most proficient attorneys know that time invested early in the process will set up the end game beautifully.

This is similar to a flawless shot off the tee in golf. A golfer spends time assessing the greens, lining up his shot, and then tees the ball up just right to hit the perfect shot.

Set yourself apart by making your first five minutes with a client meaningful and memorable.

Chapter Fifteen
The Opening And The Agenda-Setting Statement

The opening is infinitely more important than the closing! If you can open initial consultations more effectively, you can close more competently. An impressive opening to an initial consultation establishes a connection, sets the tone of the meeting, and builds trust.

It is important at the beginning to set the right tone and intention because this is the part of the meeting that elicits the most pushback and opposition from prospects, as they don't know what you intend to do to them. They think that you are going to try to close them, push things forward, and go in for the kill. They are in protection mode.

It is up to you diffuse the pressure and get people to open up and tell you the truth. People who like, trust, and respect you will listen to you. If not, they may lie to you.

There are dozens of ways to craft an opening statement. Make it your own. Choose your words carefully. Be genuine. If your statement sounds like a series of canned words coming out of your mouth, the client will sense and feel it. If your statement sounds robotic and scripted and does not come from an authentic place, you are done.

The process that you are about to create for your practice must be easily modifiable so that it may be used in the variety of selling situations that you will most likely face. There is no one-size-fits-all approach. Each client and situation is so different that to expect one approach to work for all of them is unrealistic.

You may find yourself having an informal initial encounter with a potential client, a face-to-face formal presentation, a simple fact-finding meeting, or a complimentary consultation. Keep in mind that every situation is different and that every client is an individual, and one statement will not work for all situations.

Your agenda-setting statement is the transition from pleasantries and light banter to the reason for the meeting. I call it a bridge statement. It's the bridge that you must cross that signals that you are moving from chit-chat to the heart of the meeting.

You owe it to your prospect to show respect for his time by clearly and concisely stating the purpose of the conversation. This is important because respect and trust make someone more comfortable sharing the personal and valuable information that you need to develop a solution that satisfies his needs and wants.

Start every meeting with a concise statement of what you propose to accomplish. It is your job at the beginning of the conversation to let your prospective client know how your time together will be spent, how long the meeting will last, and what is on the agenda. By agenda, I do not mean your personal agenda. I am referring to the agenda for what you're there to discuss.

Once you have opened with your agenda-setting statement, the remainder of the conversation should be collaborative. It is a dialogue not a monologue. Your job is to make sure that you are both on the same page from beginning to end.

Set The Intention And Maintain Control Of The Conversation

Without some ground rules and an agenda, the meeting may get away from you. Someone has to take charge, but not in a controlling way. Taking charge makes you look like a leader, a strong attorney, and respectful of someone else's time. Plus, it lends you the credibility that you need to get the prospect to open up and talk to you.

Creating the content of your own personal agenda-setting statement will be up to you. Devise one that fits you and your personality. Use the example below as a template for your agenda-setting statement. Remember, this statement must leave your lips with ease and flair. Practice your statement until it is perfect.

Example 1: Susan, I'm glad that we were able to meet to discuss the details of your situation and how I may be able to help you. I know that when we set up our appointment, we blocked out about an hour. Will that timeframe still work for you?

Based upon what you shared with me on the phone, I think that I may be able to assist you. We will get to that in a few minutes. In order for us to explore whether we might work well together, we will need to discuss your challenges and goals a bit more thoroughly.

Susan, my purpose is to understand, not assume, how these challenges are affecting you, so I have some specific questions to ask you that will help me better understand your particular situation. I know that you will have some questions for me as well.

Depending upon your circumstances and the information that we gather today, it may make sense for you and I to delve into some options and possible solutions.

Before I get into who I am and what I do, could you briefly describe the specifics of your situation and why you need to hire an attorney. Then, if I think that I can help you, we will discuss the next step.

Side bar: Notice that I used the words *briefly describe the specifics of your situation*. You are communicating to the prospect that a short description is all you need. This is not an opportunity for your prospect to drone on and on. It is an opportunity for you to shine the spotlight on her and listen to what is said, and what is not said.

Example 2: Anthony, when you called to schedule your initial consultation with our intake manager, Stephanie, she shared with you that initial client meetings like this may take up to an hour. Is that still okay with you?

I will need some time to ask some questions that will allow me to understand the specifics of your situation. Plus, I want to give you the opportunity to ask questions of me and make sure you understand how I can help you. Together we can discuss next steps and look at options if you choose to move forward.

In my review of your intake form, it looks like you are having difficulty with X and Y and need to do some exploration around Z. I know you understand that my firm handles these types of cases, so before I discuss how I may help you, I'd like to start by asking you to briefly...

Using an agenda-setting statement is one way to differentiate yourself and allows the prospect to experience you as someone who cares, listens, and does not feel the need to start the meeting talking about themselves. The bonus for you is that while your prospect is talking to you, she is becoming more at ease. She is feeling more comfortable. Remember, comfortable people buy. You control the dial of their comfort.

This type of agenda-setting statement accomplishes a lot in a short amount of time. It sets you apart. It spells out exactly what will happen during your time together.

This is a radically different approach than most attorneys use. While other attorneys lull prospects to sleep with their typical boring and self-serving opening, you immediately show them that you are different and focused on helping and hearing them. Keep in mind that the prospect may not consciously know how or why you are different. Their gut and intuition tells them that you are, that you are not like the other attorneys that they've spoken to, that you are not like the last firm they met with. These feelings happen on the unconscious level, the level in which people make their buying decisions.

Every initial meeting should start with an agenda-setting statement of this kind. Failing to start a meeting with a statement like this will result in lost opportunities and revenue. Neglecting to set the tone, energy, and intention of a meeting may lead to a meeting that goes off the rails and becomes difficult to save.

The agenda-setting statement idea in my coaching programs is where I receive the most eye rolling, foot stomping, and pushback from attorneys. They don't understand why they can't begin a meeting the way they always have, talking about themselves. They have been doing it this way for so long that change is not welcome. I tell these attorneys that it is not about them and that they need to check their ego at the door when meeting new prospects. Your ego is not needed in this meeting. Your prospects will be impressed, and they will leave you feeling heard.

Warning! Be careful with this approach. This new and modern way to communicate might lead to a wealth of new business and additional clients. Try it. It works!

You will no longer worry about your initial meetings because you'll know where to keep the focus, which is on the client. This contributes to your confidence, and your stress will dissipate. You will find opening conversations effortless. You'll have a new comfort level around communicating because you're focused on the client and not on your own concerns and goals.

You will mesmerize people with your conversations. They will be drawn to you because you're addressing a specific problem that is of concern to them. You come across as relaxed and natural. Your conversations lead others to trust you, which makes it easier for people to open up so that you may learn the truth about their situation. When you set aside your own agenda and focus 100 percent on prospective clients, trust grows and the truth emerges.

If the client presses you for information about you or your firm, make the point succinctly. Satisfy his request, but don't slip into a full-blown soliloquy about yourself or the firm.

Keep Your Mind Off Of The Close And Closing Too Soon

I receive calls every day from attorneys asking me if I can teach them how to close, if I can teach them some new closing techniques. They believe that the only skill they lack is how to close. They're convinced that that is the one thing missing in their process. They assume that they're not closing the sale because they lack that magical phrase, that slick one-liner, or some fancy closing statement. What that tells me is that the wheels came off a few miles back and that we need to turn around and find out where.

There is no secret sentence, no magical phrase, no covert closing technique that transforms a law practice or increases revenue. What will transform your practice is when you are willing to take your mind off of the close and put your focus on how a meeting begins.

Chapter Sixteen
What's Trust Got To Do With It?

Knowing how to develop sincere trust is essential to expanding your practice. Trust is the single most important prerequisite for creating client relationships that produce monumental results with less time and effort. Earning and maintaining trust must be approached deliberately.

Trust does not depend on the length of time that two people have known each other. Trust depends on the depth of understanding that develops between them. Your reputation for being trustworthy is something that you strengthen over time with a consistent, positive performance.

Your prospects are coming to the table with a little less trust than in the past. Unfortunately, these days some attorneys make promises that they don't keep. The bar on trust is set low, and you can actively work to raise the level.

Your clients will likely decide within the first few minutes of talking to you whether you're the type of person/attorney that they want to do business with. We size people up based on the way they communicate with us, and we do this quickly. It all comes down to whether someone trusts you.

Your potential clients not only listen with their ears, they also observe with their eyes.

You may be the most honest attorney on the planet, but if your clients don't perceive you to be trustworthy, it doesn't matter.

Do not *say* that you are client-focused, *be* client-focused. Do not *say* that you are trustworthy, *be* trustworthy.

In today's highly competitive marketplace, your clients have many options, and they're looking for an attorney whom they know they can trust to work in their best interests. Being conscious of this will help you to establish a firm foundation from which you may effectively conduct your business.

Knowing, understanding, and possessing the traits that clients need is the best way to gain trust and seal the deal. In addition to being honest, you need to be knowledgeable, punctual, solution-based, and customer-focused. It's the way that you relate to others that determines your client's level of trust.

We all buy from people whom we trust. That's why it's so important to take the time to build chemistry and rapport, quickly and sincerely, throughout your process. Make it a priority.

Before you pick up the phone to call a prospect or sit down to an initial meeting with someone, make sure that you plan to earn trust by design, not default. Make sure that you will be able see things from the other person's point of view. Your prospects should leave a meeting with you thinking, *She is a fantastic listener. He can help us with our business issues. She made me feel comfortable and put me at ease, and I can see myself working with that firm.*

If you keep in mind your prospect's desires, you will both walk away from a meeting in a better place. All parties are happy.

Rapport And Trust

There is a fine line but a clear distinction between rapport and trust, but this is often missed by inexperienced attorneys. Understanding both will put you in a stronger position to make rain.

Rapport has three components: compassion, connection, and credibility. Think of each of these as a building block in the foundation of your business success. Rapport sets the tone of the relationship between you and a prospective client. With a strong and solid foundation, you can grow and maintain beneficial client relationships.

Trust also has three components: competence, commitment, and consistency. The taller the building, the deeper the foundation required. That means delivering on your promises. Each time you do, the foundation becomes more solid. Trust translates to a prospect having confidence that you will do what you say you're going to do.

Think of this as it relates to the dating world. You meet someone for the first time. You notice that they're working way too hard to impress you and get you to like them. They agree with everything you say, look you in the eyes while smiling, and hang on your every word. This overkill makes you feel uncomfortable and uneasy. It's too much too soon, and trying too hard is a glaring sign of desperation. This approach ends up backfiring because forcing rapport and trust feels unnatural.

It's hard to trust someone when they are trying too hard. On the flip side, when you meet someone for the first time and things are going well, the atmosphere feels friendlier and more relaxed. You almost start to feel the trust developing, and the conversation flows lighter and easier. Rapport must be established at the beginning of every relationship, whether it lasts twenty minutes or twenty years.

Think of a time when you met someone for the first time and the conversation felt natural, completely comfortable, and tension free. You could see that you were a good fit.

Client Loyalty

It's difficult, if not impossible, to acquire a loyal client without trust. Do your prospective clients trust what you say? Do they trust you as an attorney? Skilled attorneys gather information in a natural manner that instantly gets clients to engage. Talented attorneys shine the spotlight on and focus their attention on their clients.

Prospects may come to your meeting painting all attorneys with the same brush. To them, all attorneys come out of the same mold and should not be trusted. Make sure that you take the paintbrush out of their hand by acting in a manner that engenders instant trust.

When was the last time you made a sizable purchase from someone you didn't like? Or the last time you gave money to someone you were not so sure about? Chances are, almost never. The same is true for your clients. Just because someone likes you doesn't guarantee you a sale. Gaining trust and building rapport with your clients when you move through the sales process will help you close more sales and make more rain.

Chapter Seventeen
Avoiding The Commodity Trap

These days it is critical that you define and communicate what makes you different from your competition. Prospective clients will assume that you are just like your competitors until you demonstrate that you are not.

Are you being asked to lower fees to win business or discount services to keep business? If so, it means that you are being seen as a commodity, getting paid for what you do and not the value that you provide.

Ask yourself what sets your service or firm apart from your competitors? What value do you provide, and how is it different than the alternatives? Without differentiation, it takes more time, energy, and money to show prospective clients why they should hire you. You may compete on price now, but this is a tough proposition to sustain over the long term.

In today's marketplace where so many products and services are viewed as a commodity, the ability to add value to your product or service is a necessity. People don't always buy based on the lowest price any more, and few people believe that the lowest price equals the best value.

If your client does not see the value in your product or service, then any price will be too high. Demonstrate to your clients how your service will benefit them, and watch how easy the buying decision becomes.

Some clients start off asking about price. However, as you find out more about them, you will discover that other things are important to them as well: quality, speed, reputation, brand name, and service.

Think about your last trip to the grocery store. Maybe you bought a few generic items, but if you're like most people, you also walked out with a few brand-name items in your cart. Are those brand-name food items any better than their generic counterparts? In some cases maybe so. Do you ever compare ingredients between brands? If you do, you'll find that many times the ingredients are exactly the same. In fact, some brands sell their products through private labeling, and it's quite possible that the brand-name and the generic are exactly the same except for the packaging and the price. So why would anyone ever buy the brand-name item that costs more? Because it has a higher perceived value. Your practice is no different.

High Perceived Value

If you're not convinced yet, think about this: if price is the only thing that matters and people are simply looking for a bargain, no one would drive a Mercedes, Nordstrom would have no customers, and diamonds wouldn't be a girl's best friend. When you're selling anything, it's important to remember that your clients must feel that they've received their money's worth.

They'll buy when they perceive a high value. And if you make them feel that they are getting a good value when they hire you, there's a good chance that they will refer you to their family and friends.

In this highly competitive sales environment, attorneys find it difficult to differentiate their service from their competitors in any way but price, but price-cutting is a losing proposition. This dilemma is faced by all businesses, whether one is selling sophisticated high-tech products, real estate, or a service of some kind.

If having the lowest price is the model for your business, go ahead and sell on price. But if it's not, you need to disqualify clients who want the lowest price and spend your time formulating the value that you want to deliver.

Your competitors say that they have similar offerings. They say that they have the same features and produce the same benefits. They look like you. They sound like you. They provide the same product or service as you, and they are cheaper. Now what?

To break out of the price trap, you must work extremely hard at differentiating your offering as it relates to results and to the return on investment. Spend your time learning to offer more value than your competitors, and focus on showing how you can create better outcomes.

Clients do not buy a remarkable service simply because it is a remarkable service. Clients buy a remarkable service because of what that service will do for them.

Perhaps the lackluster sales results you have experienced are not because of your unreasonably high prices and your misfortune at only finding clients with no money, but rather they are due to poor or messy selling skills and forgetting to sell value. An immediate tune-up is necessary.

Chapter Eighteen
It's Never About Fees, It's Always About Value

The most common objections attorneys hear are, *Your rate is high. These fees are not in our budget. Your firm is too expensive.* This may come as a surprise, but when a client objects to price, **it's never about the money**. It's actually a glaring symptom of a much larger issue in your process.

Clients use the money objection because they don't know what else to say. It's been used on people for years, and it's the easiest way to get you to retreat. The money objection constructs a protective barrier around the client so that she may hide from making a decision or from telling you no.

Any of the above excuses are default excuses and client code for *no or not right now*. It's your job to decode and translate what the excuse means. When he tells you that he cannot afford your services, it may mean any number of things. It may mean that he doesn't want to go to the trouble to change firms, so that is his excuse for ending the conversation. Or it may mean that she knows that she needs to hire an attorney, but the investment is outside of her comfort zone. It could mean that he can't see the value in your offering. You must uncover the real reason that a prospect is creating a diversion.

Prospective clients are afraid to part with their money. Money equals security, and it doesn't matter whether you're asking them to part with $19.95 or $1,995. People are happy to spend their money when they see that there's more value in using your services than in keeping their money.

This is where your value comes in. An attorney who handles DUI cases explains to her prospective client all sides of the legal issues. The good, the bad, and the ugly. This includes the differences between hiring her or allowing a public defender to defend him.

While the initial investment in hiring counsel may seem high, the cost of not having wise counsel could cost even more in the end. For example, Alex must think about the consequences of being convicted of a DUI versus having a reputable attorney by his side at trial. A strong attorney may work with the prosecutor to have one or more of the charges dropped or to get the case dismissed altogether. This saves Alex a lot of money in the long run and major headaches in the process.

On the other hand, while public defenders are legal professionals, they are often overworked with heavy caseloads, and many times a defendant may not get the one-on-one attention that he deserves. Worse yet, some individuals choose to go through the trial alone. That means that they may go to jail, pay a heftier fine, and possibly lose their driver's license for a time, which means that working and earning a living would be difficult. The investment in hiring a competent attorney outweighs the cost of not hiring one.

It is a common fallacy that people buy based on price. Some do, but most people buy based on value or their perception of value. Some attorneys start their practice with the thought that they'll enter the market and simply offer what they have at a lower price and their business will do fine. They soon see how false that is.

Tip The Value Scale

In virtually every buying situation, the customer visualizes an imaginary set of scales or balances in his mind. In the decision-making process, prospects use those scales to weigh the value of the product or service being considered. What happens in too many cases is that attorneys do an ineffective job of presenting the specific benefits of the service that they offer. They fail to show the client how he will be much better off after hiring them or procuring their services.

When this happens, the value of what you deliver and bring to the table is not seen. Your clients get their *value* scales out and quickly determine the benefits that they would receive versus the money that they would be required to spend.

This is precisely the moment where the weighing game begins in your client's mind. If the value does not exceed the price and the benefits don't outweigh the cost, the objections start to fly.

If the prospective client feels that what you describe is exactly what they think they can get from a less expensive attorney or online legal services, they will not retain you. To them, they perceive the value in your offering as just like the guy down the street, or worse, the same as an online legal service such as LegalZoom.

Adding value to your product or service is an absolute necessity. There is no doubt that in the absence of value, virtually any product or service may be driven down to one thing, price.

Chapter Nineteen

The Lost Art Of Follow-Up

Following up and following through are a critical part of the process but sadly have become the most neglected and underused tool in the business tool box. There are many reasons why sales are lost, but one of the major reasons is poor or no follow-up. Neglecting to finish what you've started shows a lack of attention on your part to your prospective clients.

Attorneys who are serious about their practice follow up and follow through. The question isn't how many opportunities you make each week, it's how many you lose.

When it comes to follow-up, do you do what you say you're going to do, when you say that you will do it? Or do you speak the words but never follow through? Not following up is an epidemic today, and this form of self-sabotage is completely within your control. You chose not to do what you needed to do. You fully participated in forgetting, running out of time, and getting sidetracked. There is no such thing as a good excuse, only a well-thought-out lie.

Of course, sometimes things happen, or in a rare instance you do forget, but I am not talking about an occasional incident, I'm talking about blatant business neglect.

Think of a situation where you started a discussion with someone that you thought about doing business with. You took phone calls, participated in meetings, or exchanged e-mails and then got to the part where you were ready to give them your business, but they never asked, or they disappeared entirely. They completely dropped the ball. They left you surprised at their behavior and disappointed that they wasted your precious time.

It shocks me that some attorneys run their business this way. And they're the ones complaining that things are rough out there. Of course it's tough when you drop the ball, neglect prospective clients, and then choose to not finish something you started. Remember, there's no good excuse for not following through or following up. If you ever utter the words, I forgot, I ran out of time, or I will do it tomorrow, you're pressing down hard on the brakes of your business.

A good follow-up system will keep sales moving and keep your business in business. It's an investment that you can't afford not to make if you want to stay ahead of your competition. Clients respect efficient, organized, and dedicated business owners and professionals who follow through. When you follow up, you win clients.

Since few professionals follow up properly with clients, you will truly stand out when you do. Clever attorneys write things down, have a system in place to handle daily to-do tasks, return calls, keep their promises, and do what they say they will do.

In the business world there are those who think about it and talk about it, and then there are those who do it. I challenge all attorneys, for twenty-one days, to stop talking about what they need to do and simply do it. If you say that you will call someone back, call them back. If you RSVP for an event, go to the event, don't pull a no-show. If you say that you will e-mail someone, send the e-mail. If you tell someone that you will take care of something, take care of it. Honor your word. Follow up and follow through.

Follow-up is a key to scoring in any business. Unfortunately, there are attorneys who ignore this critical business step and consequently leave money on the table. Give yourself an instant raise and follow up!

Not Following Up Is Costly

Actions speak louder than words. People must stop talking about following up and start doing it. Failure to follow up happens in every industry, every day, and it affects all of us personally and professionally. With this type of negligence, it's not surprising that so many attorneys are not making much rain.

If you willingly let your clients fall through the cracks due to a lack of organization, failure to follow through, or poor communication, you may jeopardize the sale, your professional reputation, and the potential for referrals. Poor communication or lack of responsiveness is a leading reason why clients leave businesses for a competitor. Being diligent in following up is an immediate way to generate more sales.

There is a disconnect in business between what people say and what they do. Think about how much time, money, and energy you've put into developing strategies, networking, and advertising. Dropping the ball at the follow-up stage sends a message to clients that they can't count on you. This is not only unprofessional, it is bad business. Is that the first impression that you want to leave with your potential clients?

Chapter Twenty

Don't Overcome Objections, Handle Them Instead

Why do you hear objections? What do they mean? From here on out, learn to treat objections as if a prospect is saying, *I am not sold on the details that you've presented so far. Could you please give me more information so that I might make an educated decision?* Your prospect needs more from you so that she may confidently say yes.

Objections that you'll come across include: *Your fees are too expensive. This won't work for me. This all sounds too complicated. This is going to be too hard to accomplish. Now is not the right time.*

When you get an objection, all you have to do is acknowledge it, diffuse it, and address a prospect's concerns around the objection. Don't utter a snappy comeback. Understand what the client is saying. When you do, your conversations will remain comfortable and authentic, which is what prospects always want in the end.

When a potential client gives you any kind of objection, most of the time they're telling you that they're interested, but there is something standing in the way of saying yes. Objections may arise from a client who wants his doubts clarified, or he needs further information or reassurance about certain points. People don't ask questions and have objections unless they are seriously considering you and your service.

View the objection as a request for more information or as a prospect's concern or fear. Every objection provides you with a new opportunity to share the right information with a prospect and to move them into the next step of your sales process.

When a client voices a concern, never interrupt her and jump in and overcome the objection. The more she talks, the more comfortable she will feel with you, and the more you will learn about concerns that she has. Make it a point to never disagree, because that will alienate the client by proving that you think she is wrong. You may win the war of words, but you will lose the sale.

Let's face it. Buying can be a scary step. People will have legitimate concerns. It is an important part of your job to help prospects work through these fears and concerns. Your job isn't to overcome objections. Your job is to help your client be strong, be clear, and stay focused so that she can do what's right for her.

How you view and handle objections may have a significant impact on the outcome of the conversation. You can't work around objections, ignore them, or pretend that they are not there. There is a barrier between you and your prospect, and together you need to take it down. Be mindful of this. Recognize your tendency to feel defensive, and replace this with empathy and curiosity.

If you pressure someone, they'll stop trusting you. A loss of trust always means the loss of the sale. But if someone makes himself vulnerable by expressing objections and you listen and don't attack, he relaxes, remains open, and feels safe. And you may move forward without a hitch or hindrance.

If you keep yourself centered and calm instead of becoming fearful or confrontational, you then may diffuse the objection and re-open the sales conversation. This in turn allows you to help your prospective client be truthful about his situation so that he doesn't feel threatened. He needs to feel sure that if he makes himself vulnerable with you, you won't take advantage of the information that he shares and try to hard-sell him your solution.

Objection! Just the word makes some people shudder. Why? Because it could mean that rejection is coming. Or it could mean that opportunity is on the way.

Your reaction to objections has a giant impact on your ability to work through the objection to the satisfaction of your client.

During your initial consultations, it is common that some sort of objection will come up. Think of it as a concern or a question about the fit of the solution or the next step.

When an objection is stated, both parties have a stake in the outcome. How you handle the objection, not overcome it, may make or break what happens next. Most people have a fight-or-flight response to an objection.

Client Objection: *We would really like to move forward and start working with you, but your fees are much higher than two other attorneys that we are considering.*

The typical old-school response: *Well, they are both good attorneys, but neither one of them specializes in X and Y. They are not experts in your exact situation. My fees are worth it because I will provide you with excellent this and momentous that... Blah, blah, blah.*

All of this sounds to the prospective client like a mammoth justification, not a compelling reason why your fees are higher. It is your job to get underneath the objection and gain a better understanding of her objection.

My suggested response: I *appreciate you telling me that I am your top choice and that you would like to retain me. However, it sounds like my higher fees are a stumbling block and that you would like to discuss them a bit more? Is that correct?*

Let's take a step back and re-visit some of the specialized services that you are looking for and how I deliver them. Then we can talk about how those fees specifically work into the overall plan. How does that sound?

Next time you hear an objection, don't panic and think that you have to fight back and go into justification mode. Go into problem-solver mode instead. Below are three steps that you may use to handle any objection.

1. Acknowledge the objection.
2. Probe for clarity.
3. Answer with relevant information.

As you enter into any sales dialogue, you may encounter objections. Don't fear them. Don't allow them to derail the conversation. Meet them head-on using your new three-step plan.

Chapter Twenty-One
Asking For The Business And Closing The Sale

The following statements say it all when it comes to asking for the business and closing the sale. *If you don't ask, you don't get. If you don't go after what you want, you'll never have it. If you don't ask, the answer is always no. If you don't step forward, you'll stay in the same place.*

It is your job to ask for the business! Prospects don't always come out and say, *Sounds good, lets get started. I want to retain you right now*. No matter how interested they are, they are waiting for you to ask.

Not only have you earned the right to ask, you must ask. Asking for the sale is like running to first base after hitting a line drive. It's expected. If you don't make the move, you will confuse everyone involved.

Asking for the sale is the most avoided question in the sales cycle, but it is one of the most formidable. For many attorneys, closing is the hardest part of the process. They know that they have to ask, but the fear of asking stops them dead in their tracks. It's too uncomfortable to ask. They know better but often skip that step because of how it makes them feel.

Not asking for the sale, especially if someone is a good prospect, is awkward. Think about how uncomfortable your client feels when you take up all of his time, discuss what you can do for him, share information about your services, and then don't bother to ask for the business. While you're busy thinking about you and how uncomfortable you are, you never give a thought to how uncomfortable your client feels.

Think about that for a minute. You're so consumed with how you feel when you must ask for the sale that you don't consider how your prospect feels.

The client is expecting you (if it's the right fit) to ask for the business, and asking is a natural progression in the sales process. Not making an attempt to close, or asking for the business, is awkward and may cause the client to doubt you or your services. If clients can read nervousness or stiffness in your body language, you won't close the sale. Your body language may close the sale for you, or it may be a sign that you loathe asking for the business, which then becomes another lost opportunity. If you don't get comfortable asking for the sale, you may need to get comfortable with clients going to your competition.

Closing is the logical conclusion to an effective client conversation. Closing is the natural occurrence when you have completed all the steps of the sales process. It is in the close where your efforts are rewarded.

If you think that selling or closing is pushy or aggressive, you must let that go. Delete from you mind the stereotypical perceptions of a closer and what it means to close the sale. Let go of thinking that you need to be aggressive, forceful, or pushy. If you feel that you must be hawkish or offensive, your approach needs a shift. Good closing skills have nothing to do with hard sells, pushy sales people, or well-rehearsed one-liners.

Many closing strategies have been around for decades. These strategies either no longer work like they used to or can rub prospects the wrong way. Wise and savvy prospective clients have heard them all.

Closing is actually easy and effortless when you have one or two unique closes of your own. Create the language that you are most comfortable with that reflects your personality and style so that you may win the business.

It's closing time. You've done it all: prospected, qualified, presented, handled objections, discussed fees, and talked about next steps. The only thing left to do is close the sale. Stalling, resisting, fearing, and attempting to shy away from this step will guarantee another lost sale.

Unless you complete the last step, you're not done, you didn't score, you didn't finish what you started. It's no different than taking all day to prepare a wonderful meal and then not eating it.

Think of it this way. All you are doing when you ask for the sale is giving your client a gentle nudge in the direction of saying yes or no. You never have to put anyone in a headlock, paint them into a corner, or tackle them to the ground to make a decision. You are simply asking.

I don't want to force someone to work with me. What? Who said anything about forcing someone to hire you? If you have to use force, you're approach is all wrong.

I've also had a client tell me that she didn't want anyone to think that she was selling something. Really? You're not fooling anyone pretending that you are not selling something. You are, and everyone knows it. It's time to drop the disguise and be the noteworthy attorney behind your noteworthy service and expertise.

Wishing, hoping, and praying for the sale is not nearly as effective as asking for the sale. One of the things that you can do at the end of the meeting or at the end of the call, after you have done all the hard work, is to maintain the momentum that you started in the process by setting up what I call the next steps. You have the obligation to ask your client for some type of commitment. This looks different with each individual client, and you must keep the momentum going.

Watch and listen for buying signals. Buying signals are a prospect's way of pointing out that they have enough information or interest in you or your services and are ready for the next step. That next step may be hiring you or scheduling another meeting.

These signals may be subtle verbal signals, such as: Oh! Hmm! They may be direct or obvious: We would work well together. This seems like an easy process! And these signals could fall anywhere in between.

Now you have what appears to be a buying signal. The purpose of the meeting has been achieved. It's time to stop talking about your service and move the process forward!

You must close all the way from beginning to end. Perhaps you closed a gatekeeper to get the prospect on the phone. You closed the prospect by getting the first appointment, closed her on enticing her to tell you her problems or desires and on wanting to know your solution, closed her on being willing to listen to you and answer your questions, perhaps closed on a follow-up appointment or call, and then closed her on agreeing that you or your services can solve her problem.

You're now at the next step, getting a yes, a no, or a maybe. There are countless ways to ask for the business. Getting to this point and stopping the momentum is going to have to be a thing of the past. It is not your client's job to indicate to you that he is ready to get started or is ready to work with you. It's your job to make something happen next. All you have to do is ask.

The whole process is a series of closes that ends with one final close. The final close occurs, and the selling process is complete, when the prospect agrees to hire you and arranges payment.

Below are just a few examples of ways to ask for the business. The list below should be a good starting point for you. If the meeting is going well, pull out your audacity and ask:

- What are your thoughts on moving forward?
- Where would you like to go from here?
- What would you like our next step to be?

- Based on what we talked about, how do you feel about taking the next step?
- Based on what we talked about, how do you feel about hiring our firm?
- Based on what you shared with me, it seems like a good fit. What do you think about moving ahead?
- If we decide to move forward, perhaps we could talk about what happens next. Are you comfortable with that?
- Based on what you know about my firm, are you comfortable moving forward?

Asking for the business using a fresh and modern approach like the above is more effective for you and feels better for the client.

Using outdated, stale, and predictable lines like those found below do nothing to differentiate you.

- I think that we should sign the paperwork and move forward.
- Is there anything that you can think of that would keep us from working together?
- If I could show you a way to save money, would you consider doing business with our firm?
- Do you feel that you have everything you need to make a decision today?

The answer to these closing statements and questions usually results in prospects saying, *Let me think about it. I will call you next week.* Prospects may feel confronted with this kind of language and may feel forced into making an immediate decision.

It's your job to close and to find a way to do it that feels right for you. All parties involved should know exactly what is going to happen next. Moving forward with complete clarity on both sides, making sure that everyone is on the same page, is an effective and efficient way to do business.

I see too many individuals get to this point in the process, and they ask for the business, but they use feeble, banal closes. Some attorneys close by saying things such as: *Well, let me know when you want to get started. Give me a call when you're ready. Keep me posted as to when the time is right for you.*

This may sound like a close, but it is not. It is not firmly asking for the business. By simply changing the way that you ask for the business, you will automatically increase your closing percentage.

That's it! It's that simple. Taking the initiative to close the business shows confidence, strength, and power. It shows that you believe in you and your service.

Chapter Twenty-Two

Networking Like A Pro: Turning Your Contacts Into Connections

Networking is a productive way to build professional relationships and find new business opportunities. Networking is a reciprocal process based on the exchange of ideas, advice, and referrals. Having a networking strategy is invaluable.

It's often been said that if you don't know where you're going, any road will get you there. The same is true of your network and professional relationships. When attempting to increase the number of your business relationships, having a networking strategy will make your efforts more effective and efficient.

Some of the stellar rainmakers that I have worked have allowed me to share with you below the networking mantras that work for them:

1. I will build my network and relationships with consistency, intensity, and enthusiasm.
2. My network is my top priority, and I will devote significant effort to expanding my network.
3. Cultivating new relationships is not just something to add to my to-do list, I will add it to my must-get-done list.
4. Expanding my network and relationships is no longer on the back-burner for me. I will actively pursue new business and nurture relationships as they grow and strengthen.

5. I will put energy into meeting and interacting with people during the course of my business activities. I will work proactively to build my network and relationships.

Smart networkers know how to work a room! Productive networkers know how to convert their connections into clients and close deals.

Strong networkers are easy to spot. They circulate with grace and ease, meeting, greeting, and talking to people in a way that looks and sounds sincere. It's obvious that they know how to start, develop, and end lively and interesting conversations that enhance rapport.

Working a room like a pro means having many short conversations with many people. Short doesn't mean superficial. It's entirely possible to have thought-provoking, meaningful, and stimulating short conversations with new contacts that yield connections and make you memorable.

Many attorneys attend networking events with good intentions of meeting people and cultivating new relationships. Not everyone goes with the same good intentions. Some are only attending to hunt for prey and seem more interested in stalking others and finding new victims.

Networking isn't about hunting for prospects, it's about making contacts that eventually lead to a connection. The networker who works a room with a *what's in it for me* attitude will never find new clients.

Working a room is not about buzzing around and pressing your cards into the palms of anyone with a free hand. Networking is not about haphazardly having fleeting half-conversations with other people. Sure, you will meet a lot of people if you do this, but it is highly unlikely that you will make an impact. If you do, it won't be a favorable one.

For many, networking comes naturally. For others it has to be learned and continuously honed. Not everyone gets excited or enjoys attending networking events. Like it or not, you have to do it. Yes, it may be uncomfortable walking into a room full of people you don't know, but this is not an excuse for skipping this business-building activity.

When you know how to work a room, you feel better about yourself, you make many social and business contacts, and you make others feel more comfortable too. Your particular way of being will attract people to you and make them want to know you better.

Next time you are at an event, make a conscious decision to approach people to whom you might not normally speak. Armed with your repertoire of conversation-starters and questions, you should have no difficulty in making a good first impression and developing rapport. The more people you meet in a genuine way, the less fazed you will be by the networking process. It's all part of the big networking plan of effectively working a room.

Below are a few conversation starters to open up dialogue and suggestions to keep the conversation going:

- What types of projects are you working on right now?
- Are you working on anything exciting?
- What are your plans for this weekend?
- Are you staying in town for the holidays?
- What types of networking events do you enjoy going to?
- What do you like to do in your spare time?
- Have you been to an event like this before?
- How long have you been involved in this organization?
- Is this a busy time for you?

Have a few go-to questions that feel right for you in your mind ahead of time.

Another important tip to remember when you are working a room is to not be in sales mode. Move gently from social to business conversation and avoid any appearance of selling. People aren't at networking events to buy or be sold, they're there to network.

You must network if you want to grow your business and get more referrals. You must be willing to have interesting conversations with many new people. I tell my clients that unless their phone is ringing off the hook and they have more business than they can handle, they must be networking on a regular basis.

Get out there and work the room like the pros. It is one of the best ways to grow your practice.

Network Your Way To Success

Many business professionals today believe that *who you know* is just as important as *what you know*. Doing business certainly relies as much on people skills as on qualifications and experience. You may find it more difficult to achieve the prosperity that you deserve if your skill set is unbalanced, loads of one and not much of the other.

No matter how brilliant you are or how much you know about the law, if you want to get ahead, good connections will help. Getting to know people and making new connections is an essential part of growing your practice and making rain.

One important thing to remember while networking is that it helps to be curious about other people. They'll find you far more interesting if you show an interest in them. Learning the fine art of networking is not about you.

> *You can make more friends in two months by becoming interested in other people than you can in two years by trying to get other people interested in you.*
>
> ~ Dale Carnegie

Being generous and courteous to others makes you memorable and is a wonderful networking asset.

As you begin to network, the key will lie in your ability to be flexible. Everyone is familiar with the saying, *If you do what you've always done, you'll get what you've always got.*

Using the same approach over and over again in networking will not produce results. And why should it? No one person is the same as another, so why should repeating the same introductory remarks and conversational opening statements be right for every contact and occasion? Be flexible and genuine.

Be confident and become adept at trying new approaches, and you will succeed. Once you get used to networking and begin to make progress with relationship-building, the motivation to continue will be high.

Those who enjoy networking find it fun and exciting. For those who don't enjoy networking, it may be daunting and scary. But it is the best way to overcome shyness, discover unexpected opportunities, increase sales, and develop new relationships.

You may be feeling reluctant to take the first steps, whether from fear or lack of time, but a positive outlook is vital to relationship-building. Once you learn how to make connections in a way that feels comfortable for you, you'll overcome shyness and get excited about networking. Once you have broken down the barriers that up to this point have prevented you from trying, you'll feel completely different.

Be interested in others rather than forcing others to be interested in you. When you are generous to those you meet, you will find the motivation to identify opportunities through your positive mental attitude.

When Your Networking Isn't Working!

Effective networking helps you to find new clients, helps you to reinforce relationships, and helps you to improve sales. Poor networking costs you sales, reduces referrals, and produces dismal results for your business.

The main reason why people fail at networking is that they have never been taught how to do it properly.

The Top Five Networking Mistakes That Attorneys Make

1. **Handing out business cards before introducing yourself.** Networking is not about one-way advertising, it's about relationships. Don't push your business card on people and hope that they will be enamored by you and want to do business with you. People form relationships with people, not with business cards. Networking is not about the number of cards that you hand out, it is about the quality of the people that you connect with.
2. **Monopolizing the conversation.** When you meet someone for the first time, do you ramble on about your business,

or do you ask about hers? Find out a little more about what she does instead of monopolizing the conversation. Asking someone about her business is a good way to stop this kind of bad networking behavior. It is important to engage with others in order to build strong connections.

3. **Being phony.** Everyone knows when someone is schmoozing them. No one likes a head-nodding phony who only appears to be interested. There is a big difference between acting interested and being genuinely interested. When you are interested in learning about another person and his business, you will leave a lasting good impression.

4. **Adding people to your mailing list without their permission.** It amazes me how many people think that it is okay to send others their newsletter and/or promotional e-mails just because someone gave them their business card. If you want to put someone on your list, you must ask their permission first. Send a new connection an e-mail asking if she would like to receive your newsletter. Let her know that it is okay to decline.

5. **Not listening.** Most people can tell when another person is tuning them out. Being a good listener is the sign of a great networker. If you want the same courtesy, you must listen to the other person. This is the Law of Reciprocity at its finest. When someone is speaking, give that person your full attention. The best gift that you can give to another person is to listen and truly hear their words.

It is not what you know or even who you know. It is how well you know someone and how well they know you that really matters in constructing a dominant network.

Chapter Twenty-Three

Using Social Media Marketing And Technology To Increase Your Presence And Grow Your Practice

If you're like many professionals these days, you have more than a little trepidation about entering the digital and social marketplace. In today's ever-changing technological age, it may be overwhelming to keep up with current trends. It is normal to have some anxiety around being new at using such a powerful tool. I promise that getting started is the only hard part.

Social media and technology have leveled the playing field for everyone in every industry. They have officially changed the way that people connect, communicate, engage socially, and do business. Social media and technology have transformed the world and brought forth change greater than at any other period in history. This change is so widespread that it is hard to imagine a time when we lived without the Internet, smartphones, and myriad other devices. You can't ignore this fact.

Building a prosperous practice has never been easier with the tools of technology available today. Technology enables attorneys to market their services and sell themselves without spending a fortune. If you have not embraced social media yet, run, don't walk, and join the more than 300 million people using social media. You won't regret it.

Online marketing is becoming more and more popular. You cannot afford to ignore this important fact in your practice. You may come up with a few excuses, a dozen reasons, and lots of justifications why you don't have time to market online. But none of these excuses, reasons, or justifications will hold water. A marketing attitude shift is in the making.

Along with a good marketing attitude, you need effective and solid marketing habits. It's difficult to market on a steady basis unless you have a plan or a system in place. Your goal is to develop superior marketing habits that are so automatic that you don't have to think about them.

Think of social media like a first-rate workout regimen. Those who benefit the most set aside a regular and specific time to work out. They stick with it. It becomes another natural and routine activity.

Whatever you decide about marketing your services, do it daily. Otherwise, your efforts will be difficult to track and measure. Treat your marketing endeavors as seriously as you would working with a client.

Social Media And Technology

Social media is here to stay. Now everyone can tap into the exuberance of technology and grow their practice and build business relationships. The best part of online marketing is that it is either low-cost or free.

You cannot afford to sit back and ignore the influence that online marketing and social media has had on the legal profession. What used to work no longer does. What got you to where you are today won't keep you there tomorrow. Attorneys who do not fully engage and embrace online marketing will find themselves locked out of the world's best way to grow their practice.

Sole practitioners may use social media to market themselves online and compete against much larger firms. On social media, size does not matter. The size of your firm has little to do with your visibly and credibility. The opportunities are endless for attorneys who are willing to invest time and energy in growing their online presence.

Social media keeps you *top of mind* with others. You are more likely to be considered for opportunities and business if you have a strong presence on social media. Intermittent or no presence on social media, particularly on LinkedIn, sends a negative message to your potential clients. It could be a message that you are not that serious, perhaps you are lazy, you are not technologically savvy, or your thinking has not evolved.

Social media is no longer optional. It is critical if you wish to have a thriving practice.

Free Or Low-Cost Ways To Use Social Media And Technology

- Have a presence on Facebook, Twitter, and LinkedIn.
- Write your own blog and/or contribute to other blogs.
- Write for online magazines, industry journals, or e-books.
- Host a webinar or a teleseminar on a hot industry topic or a newsworthy event.
- Send out an electronic newsletter.

The social media landscape is changing at lightning speed. Ideas available to you to grow your practice are endless. No matter what strategies you choose, make sure that you enjoy them. If social media marketing is excruciating for you, you won't do it, or when you do, you will do it with a lousy attitude, and the wrong energy will be attached to it. Your prospective clients will feel your bad mojo.

The top three social media sites for attorneys are LinkedIn, Facebook, and Twitter.

There are plenty of books, articles, classes, and resources out there to help you decide which of these sites you would like to try first. Spend some time researching the platforms that will work best for you and your practice.

Chapter Twenty-Four
Tapping Into And Using The Power Of LinkedIn

LinkedIn is the social network of choice used by professionals for networking and making connections. The main purpose of LinkedIn is to allow people to network professionally. LinkedIn is the ultimate business power tool.

Anyone can use LinkedIn, but the site is most beneficial for people looking to network online, grow their businesses, and broaden and deepen business connections.

The basic service is free. The site lets you search for and find business associates, clients, and colleagues whom you already know. You connect with them through the site, and they become part of your network.

Once you've connected with someone, you will then have access to their list of connections. This is called your extended network. You may request an introduction to people in your extended network through your mutual contact.

The trick to using LinkedIn is to not overthink the process. Stop stressing out about having to add another new something-to-learn to your to-do list. LinkedIn is an online networking tool that isn't going anywhere. If you have not yet dipped your toe in, it's not too late. I would suggest taking the plunge and familiarizing yourself with LinkedIn immediately.

A strong LinkedIn presence has become a must-have as opposed to a nice-to-have for all professionals. Using technology and mastering certain social media platforms isn't brain surgery. It is a skill that, once integrated into your practice, will help you increase your impact, influence, and income.

Because I have seen so many attorneys resist learning how to use LinkedIn, I designed a LinkedIn Boot Camp that shortens their learning curve, teaches them how to use it in their practice, and pushes them out into the online world faster than they could do it themselves.

Technology is evolving at breakneck speed. LinkedIn is becoming the supreme communication tool for professionals. Like it or not, technology has triggered irreversible changes in the way that we do just about everything. Technology has forever changed the way that business gets done.

Business as usual has officially departed. The influence that social media has had in today's society is astounding. You can no longer sit on the sidelines. You have two options: you can resist and fade away, or you can adapt and flourish.

We are in such a virtually connected world that not having a scrupulous LinkedIn profile, or even the right kind of profile, will work against you. The lack of a LinkedIn presence will make you invisible to your prospective clients. While people used to gauge the visibility and trustworthiness of an attorney or a firm through traditional means, such as how big a yellow pages ad was or word of mouth referrals, today they are doing it via technology. This is why it is so critical to develop a strong online presence.

The good news is that if you take a bit of time to learn how to use LinkedIn, it will help you grow your practice like nothing that has come before. The bad news? If you don't adapt to this fundamentally new way of doing business, you will, in all likelihood, find yourself missing opportunities.

For now, take a break, and get comfortable with the idea of using LinkedIn every day. A few minutes a day on LinkedIn, with time and commitment, will produce amazing results.

LinkedIn is an effective way to begin relationships with prospects or businesses. Once a relationship is begun, you may cultivate it and move to offline conversations. Those conversations, if nurtured properly, may turn into paying clients. Think of it this way. A relationship starts out virtually and ends with you meeting someone, possibly a new friend, in person.

Developing and learning to manage your LinkedIn presence is one of the best tools available for taking control of your professional destiny. Your competitors are already there, it's time to join them.

The goal of the site is to allow registered members to establish networks of people whom they know and trust professionally. I recommend it to all of my clients. Why? Your current and prospective clients are already there. They are looking for you to be there too.

When you meet a prospective client at an event or a business function and leave your business card with them, in all likelihood they will search for you on LinkedIn. Will you be found if they look?

You can't ignore this hard-core fact. Your potential clients will use the Internet and social media before they think about finding you another way.

People are busier than ever, and they are spending more and more time online. If they look at your LinkedIn profile and determine that you are credible and that you represent yourself and your firm well, that saves them time. Every savvy attorney that I know uses LinkedIn to learn more about the people and the companies that he or she is thinking about doing business with.

By not having a presence on LinkedIn, an attorney is telling the entire business world that he or she is not open for business. Failing to stay current will force you into professional obscurity.

If you are using LinkedIn or other social media, you must constantly ask yourself if your presence online supports your offline reputation as an attorney who is seen as an expert and as someone who may be trusted. Does your profile help your prospective clients view you as a credible resource with a trusted reputation? If you answered no, it's time for some minor adjustments or a full-blown profile makeover.

Prospects may look you up online in an effort to get a sense of who you are and what you are all about prior to meeting with you. What they find will cause them to make instant judgments about you. Those judgments will impact your ability to influence and inspire them. Most people make split-second judgments about others. Those first impressions, regardless of how valid they are, are real and cannot be overlooked.

Your LinkedIn profile is a direct reflection of you and your practice. Until your prospect meets you by phone or in person, who you are online is who you are. Invest time in developing and perfecting your LinkedIn profile, making sure that your online image casts you in the best possible light.

I once heard that in the physical world, you sometimes get a second chance to make a good first impression. In the virtual world, you have no chance of changing a negative first impression. When potential clients view the virtual version of you and don't like what they see, they find someone else.

Start by creating a professional, polished, and complete LinkedIn profile. This profile is used to network, engage, and connect with other professionals.

Unless you are looking for a job, your profile is not an acceptable place to make your profile 100 percent about you and your accomplishments. It is not a super-duper resume. It should be written so that the reader may get a clear sense of how you could help her. Think of it kind of like your personal introduction and fifteen-second commercial. Make it about the reader, and write it so that she will desire to contact you.

LinkedIn provides you with an excellent venue in which to market your services and highlight your expertise.

Next, spend some time learning how to use LinkedIn most effectively. Use the tutorials that LinkedIn offers. Start by learning the fundamentals and go from there. Then use it every day. Like the old lottery ad proclaimed, *you have to be in it to win it.* You must be using LinkedIn to get the most out of it.

Just like going to the gym once a month isn't going to make much of a difference to your body, dabbling on LinkedIn once a month isn't going to do much for your business.

By using LinkedIn consistently, you convey to your prospects that you are an attorney who is keeping up with the changing times. Perception is reality. How your prospective clients view you is critical. You have complete control over your profile and your online presence.

I stress to my clients that it makes no sense to set up a LinkedIn profile and then never use it. This is a waste of your cherished and limited time. If you want to make a bigger impact, increase your influence, and generate more income, you must schedule time for regular LinkedIn workouts.

Set up your LinkedIn profile if you do not already have one. Invest the time to complete your full profile. Go all-in and create a profile that makes you stand out, not blend in.

I will lean on the horn again here. Your profile should be about how you may help prospective clients versus being a resume of all of your accomplishments. Your prospects are screaming, *Don't just tell me that you can help me, show me how you can get it done.*

Follow The Rules Of Engagement

The rules of engagement online are exactly the same as they are offline. The same actions that work in forming fantastic in-person relationships work online as well. The same actions that annoy, irritate, and aggravate people in the real world will irritate online connections. Get to know someone before you sell to them. Do not push your services too soon or too often. Do not make your conversations all about you, your practice, your clients. I call this the *virtual sales pitch.*

Social media is social. People want to connect with real people. Take this opportunity to show off a bit of your personality. Ask questions. Be real. Add value.

Add value. What separates you from your competition is how much you share. Share your research. Highlight your knowledge, link to articles that your contacts will find useful, keep your contacts updated on your practice. Connect your contacts with others in a variety of businesses who may be a good fit.

Get The Social Fire Started

I tell my clients to keep the social fire lit, and as it burns brightly, all they need to do is throw a log on it every day to keep it stoked. You will never have to start from scratch ever again as long as you keep the fire burning.

In the beginning, social media is very time-consuming, but do not let this deter you. Spend time each day developing your LinkedIn presence. Investing ten to twenty minutes a day interacting on LinkedIn is all you need to move the needle. I spend twenty minutes in the morning and twenty minutes in the afternoon. Start now. Don't wait. Every day that you do not use social media is hurting your practice.

LinkedIn In Five Easy Steps

1. Create an account on LinkedIn at www.linkedin.com.
2. Fill out your profile completely. Include your current place of employment and contact information. Think of an attention-getting headline, and post a nice picture of yourself. Feel free to use my profile as an example: https://www.linkedin.com/in/lizwendling
3. Upload your existing contacts.
4. Join seven to ten LinkedIn groups that cater to your industry/purpose/area of interest.
5. Don't stop at the fourth step and walk away. Use this incredible tool to explode your profits.

The Last Piece Of The LinkedIn Pie

After you have posted your profile, start off with these three easy steps:

1. Reconnect with old business contacts. Search for names on LinkedIn. Many people have lost touch with a good business contact. Perhaps someone has changed companies. LinkedIn provides a great, perfectly acceptable way to reconnect.
2. Keep in touch with new and prospective clients. Where do you keep all of those business cards that you collected at networking events? Are they scattered around your office, thrown

into an old shoebox, or wasting away in a plastic card holder? If so, you are doing yourself a disservice. The best way to ensure that you will stay in touch with contacts is to connect with them on LinkedIn. You may keep the lines of communication open between visits, calls, and e-mails. Using LinkedIn is the strongest way to stay in front of the clients that you have now and the clients that you hope to have in the future.

3. Connect with fellow members of the professional organizations with which you are associated. Many organizations have also started LinkedIn groups. This is a fast and efficient way to connect with other members of these organizations to ask questions, exchange information, and get input.

The bonus reason for investing time on building a strong online presence is this. Where in the past advertising and marketing took time and money, they can now be done instantly, automatically, and at little cost. Your online message is available all the time. There's no denying the fact that online marketing is becoming more and more popular and lucrative.

This is a book about change, about doing things differently than you have in the past. Sales and marketing have experienced a profound change, courtesy of social media. You are going to have to change too.

Everyone sells something. I believe that so much that that was the title of my last book. If you are an attorney, you are in sales.

I can advise you to adapt to the changes that social media brings, but I cannot force you to do this. I will let the marketplace do that for you. Eventually, external pressure exerted by the ever-present technology changes will force you to shift the way that you think.

By the time that those of you who resist these changes are forced to adapt to them, those who proactively decided to welcome them will be far, far ahead of the pack.

Chapter Twenty-Five

Make Your Next Move ~ The Habit Of Taking Action

I have noticed that attorneys who find themselves riding on the revenue rollercoaster can't seem to get themselves to take immediate action before a situation becomes a problem. They labor to get the ball rolling in the right direction. They have told me that it feels like they are working in mud. The footsteps are heavy and slow, which makes it tough to move in any direction with strength and commitment. It's not that they don't know what to do or how to do it. The problem for them is actually doing something.

When it comes to goals and your to-do list, you might find yourself stuck in the thinking and planning phases. If you don't eventually get into action, you're wasting your time. How can you get into a sustainable mode of forward motion without feeling like you have to torture yourself? Going from thinking about what you want to making it happen is a bold move.

Success in your practice isn't determined by genetics, it's about persistent and consistent action. Action is the key. You may be the most talented person in the world or have the best ideas, but if you don't take action, you will accomplish nothing. Having goals, dreams, and passion isn't enough. You actually must do something. Don't let life happen to you. Take action now!

The rainmaking attorneys with whom I work share a strategic quality. They get things done. This is the might of **GSD** (**G**et **T**hings **D**one, or, as I like to call it, **G**et **S**hit **D**one).

The GSD ability overrides intelligence, talent, and connections in determining the money that these attorneys earn and the speed at which they succeed. These attorneys choose action over waiting, thinking, and planning. They choose action over hoping and wishing. They know that they are the only ones responsible for their personal and professional achievements.

Despite the simplicity of this concept, there is a perpetual shortage of people who excel at getting results. The habit of putting ideas into action is essential to getting things done. This is no longer a take-it-or-leave-it proposition, it's a must-have habit in business.

The action that I'm talking about isn't simply trying something for a week or a month and declaring, *It didn't work. I tried everything.* It is not going through the motions that resemble action. I'm talking about taking monster action toward your goal with persistence, consistency, dedication, and responsibility.

Giving up and stopping the flow doesn't work. Many attorneys get to a point in their business where if something doesn't work in their timeframe or doesn't pan out the way they expect, they give up too hastily. They choose to view it as a failure. Instead of stepping back to see what they could have done differently, and how they could make it better the next time, they throw in the towel and give up. They've lost the opportunity to build a success-habit along the way.

I once heard Tony Robbins say that just when you think you've tried everything, you haven't. You can always find another way. Did you do everything you could, turn over every rock, seek advice from an expert, and look at your situation from every angle? If not, then you have not tried everything. Go back and view your situation through a different lens and a fresh set of eyes. *I've tried everything* is the same thing as *I've given up trying.*

Getting from where you are to where you want to be necessitates a comprehensive evaluation of your business. Find out what you've been doing that has gotten you to your current reality. If you are not where you want to be, you haven't made the right choices or taken the right actions. Most of us don't know how to make the right choices to support our goals because we never learned how. Most of us never learned how to set goals, since goal-setting was not a class offered in school.

Some people are doers and action-takers. Some people are born thinkers and are slow to take action. Some think about doing and never get anything done. There are many ways to become a person of action.

You must know, without doubt, that taking action is the fastest, most efficient way to success. The evidence is conclusive and obvious. Action produces results, inaction produces nothing. You must decide that doing nothing will not work for you. Taking action is the only way to transformation. Inaction will destroy your business.

Action-oriented people are organized, persistent, energetic, and know exactly how to move from one project to another, effortlessly and without hesitation. Others flounder in a world of disorganization and inaction, jumping from one project to another and never working a project through to completion. The doers typically have more energy at the end of the day than they do at the beginning of the day because they feed on taking action.

There comes a point at which you need to quit thinking, researching, planning, and talking and do something! Action sparks momentum, and momentum may provide the ongoing catalyst to get you to the next step, and the next step, and the next.

Nothing matters, and nothing happens until you act. Nothing in this book will work for you unless you make the audacious decision to take action. The prosperity that you seek will be impossible unless you add a massive dose of decisive action to your repertoire. Be responsible for your life and your practice.

Business development takes time. Business development is like a crock pot, not a microwave. If you are looking for instant results, you won't find them in this book, or anywhere else for that matter. Attorneys who understand this will make more rain than they know what to do with!

The world of business has seen some tough times over the last few years, and in these challenging times, we have all grappled to come up with a magic formula, to find a blueprint that works for our singular business.

In my experience and research, there is just one equation that will allow you to achieve success in business: strong belief + firm self-discipline + unwavering commitment = exceptional abundance!

You can make rain! You can make it rain so damn much that you will be astonished. However, it is up to you to become someone with a Rainmaking Mindset so that you may reap all of the rewards that you deserve.

About The Author

Liz Wendling is a Business Development Coach, Speaker, and Author, who works with clients around the country and internationally. She is an avid golfer and spends much of her free time in the majestic Colorado mountains.

Liz's services are in demand by those who are tired of following the masses and who want to break away from the pack. She works with attorneys and other professionals who wish to take action and learn to generate tremendous results.

Whether it's next week, next month, or next year, connect with Liz about a specific tool, strategy, or idea that you ran with that made the rain come down in buckets in your world. And of course, you get all the credit because you took the leap from idea to action, and only action creates results!

In Liz's private coaching and training programs, she has assisted many individuals with the making of rain (and a hell of a lot of it!) in their professional lives.

Take the intrepid next step in being a wildly successful rainmaker. Learn the skills, tools, and tips that you need to achieve your goals. You are only an e-mail or a phone call away from Liz. She is here to give you a slight nudge or a hard shove from mediocrity to success! Discuss with her the program that works best for your individual practice. She will bring the umbrella!

Please visit www.therainmakingmindset.com to find out more about how you may become an unstoppable rainmaker.

Have Liz Speak At One Of Your Live Events

- Boosting Your Business-Development Confidence
- Making The Most Of Your Business Development
- People Buy YOU First: Show up, Stand Out, And Win More Business
- The Three Rainmaking Powers: Action, Attitudes, and Behaviors

If you wish to customize a talk for your group, I invite you to call me at 303-988-9157 or to contact me via e-mail at liz@lizwendling.com.

Made in the USA
Monee, IL
02 November 2020